1992

THE
ESSENCE
OF
LEADERSHIP

THE
ESSENCE
OF
LEADERSHIP

Strategy, Innovation, and
Decisiveness

Michel Robert

Q

QUORUM BOOKS
New York · Westport, Connecticut · London

Library of Congress Cataloging-in-Publication Data

Robert, Michel.
    The essence of leadership : strategy, innovation, and decisiveness
    /   Michel Robert.
        p.   cm.
    Includes index.
    ISBN 0–89930–655–1 (alk. paper)
    1. Leadership.   2. Industrial management.   I. Title.
    HD57.7.R63   1991
    658.4'092—dc20   91–17356

British Library Cataloguing in Publication Data is available.

Library of Congress Catalog Card Number: 91–17356
ISBN: 0–89930–655–1

First published in 1991

Quorum Books, One Madison Avenue, New York, NY 10010
An imprint of Greenwood Publishing Group, Inc.

Printed in the United States of America

The paper used in this book complies with the
Permanent Paper Standard issued by the National
Information Standards Organization (Z39.48-1984).

10 9 8 7 6 5 4 3 2 1

Contents

Preface

For the last twenty years, America has been losing the industrial competition wars. Why is this happening?

Many would argue that we are losing to the Japanese because the Japanese compete unfairly. In other words, they deliberately "close" their market to U.S. firms. However, the fact is that the biggest losses have not been to the Japanese but to the West Germans—who compete on the same basis as U.S. firms. West German products have displaced U.S. products in a larger number of market segments and a greater number of geographic markets than those of the Japanese. The British, and even the French, are starting to make significant inroads. This invalidates much of the Japan-bashing.

The cause of America's losses is that U.S. companies are being "out-thunked." Thinking has become a lost skill in American business. The concept of "fire, ready, aim" which prevails and is regarded as "macho" management is destroying America's competitive position. To illustrate this point, we have reproduced below an article by Steven H. Star, editor-in-chief of *Sloan Management Review* (Fall, 1990), which concurs with this analysis.

Midnight Musings: Rational Management in the 1990s*

The 1980s were tough for managers. Japan and Europe challenged U.S. economic dominance and global competition intensified steadily. Rapid technological change created opportunities for global parity. Social change escalated—women assumed new roles, dual-career families became the norm, and minority groups initiated legal and organizational battles for their rights. New owners radically restructured firms following mergers, acquisitions, and leveraged buyouts. All in all, conditions became rougher and rougher "out there."

These conditions demanded *rational management*. Rational management implies decision making that is systematic, analytic, creative, and ethical. It requires discipline-based thinking: rational managers are familiar with the general principles of economics, operations research, organization studies, information systems and computer science, and statistics. This approach is exactly what the MIT Sloan School and other leading business schools have been teaching for the past twenty-five years. By the 1980s, managers trained at those schools had reached positions of influence and authority. In addition, data bases were growing richer, computers less costly, and software more user friendly. By rights, rational management should have come of age in the 1980s.

Rational management has had some resounding successes, to be sure, in such areas as production and distribution logistics, financial valuation modeling, and new product forecasting. Nonetheless, the 1980s was dominated by over-simplified panaceas. ("Ready, fire, aim," however appealing, is hardly a prescription for rational management. Nor is "share maximizes profits.") What was so attractive about these cure-all approaches? Why did so many managers, confronted with crisis, turn to gurus rather than to rational management? I would say that, when the going gets really rough, there is a natural tendency to revert to the easy, the familiar and the comfortable. In other words, the primary tenets of rational management had not really taken hold for many managers.

In addition, the "go for it" approach led to overspeculation in real estate, bank failures, and a neglect of the long run, as unethical managers took advantage of newly legal opportunities. Ready-fire-aim produced a deal-making world distorted by LBOs, junk bonds, and forecasts manipulated to justify desired bidding levels. Unethical behavior magnified forecasting errors and led to clearly unacceptable and sometimes illegal acts. Mike Milken was trained at a leading business school—how could he have forgotten the lessons he should have learned? Many players in the Wall Street and S&L scandals seemed to be governed by pure, unadulterated greed.

It is my contention that we will need rational management even more in the 1990s than we did in the 1980s. All indicators suggest that the business climate will be even more rough and complex. The contributions that rational management can make will be even greater. The responsibility of those of us in academia, management journalism, and business leadership is not just to impart knowledge; it is also to change attitudes, ethical standards, and behavior.

To do this, it is necessary to overcome resistance to change on three fronts. First, managers must be persuaded of the value of rational management. Second, they need to believe in their own capacities to implement rational-management decision making effectively and appropriately. Third, they must adopt the highest standards of ethical behavior.

It won't be easy, but we've all got to get beyond simplistic generalizations and short-term thinking, and back to the basics. Back to systematic, analytic, creative, discipline-based ethical decision making. In the turbulent and challenging era we are now entering, we cannot afford to be less than the best we are capable of.

Our firm, Decision Processes International (DPI), and its sixty partners around the world have worked with over 250 corporations in some 20 countries during the last 20 years. Our work with thousands of people, from the CEO, senior executives, middle managers and even hourly personnel, has convinced us that the greatest obstacle to success is an acute inability to think on the part of a large number of these people. This difficulty is exacerbated when issues have to be resolved in a group setting. The lack of a "common language," or thinking process, is seen in dramatic fashion by the large number of erroneous conclusions arrived at in all of these major corporations.

These difficulties reflect themselves in the inability to:

- separate strategic decisions from operational ones,
- separate problem issues from decision issues,
- address the cause of a problem rather than its effects,
- assure the successful implementation of decisions by anticipating potential problems before they occur,
- distinguish between situations that require creative thinking from those that need rational analysis.

Over and over, in these 250 multinational companies, we have noticed that if these organizations had a common process of thinking that could be used by groups of people trying to resolve critical issues, that their conclusions would be significantly better. It is these processes of "critical thinking" that we are presenting in this book.

People are, indeed, creatures of habit. Unfortunately, in business today, they are creatures of bad habits, namely, the inability to think straight.

The processes you will find in this book are simply common sense. Unfortunately, common sense is not always common practice.

Good reading!

1

Modern Times

If Charlie Chaplin were alive today, he would be pleased to remind us that his view of a changing world is as valid today as it was sixty years ago. In fact, many of the trends he explored in his classic movies are still with us today, only they are happening more quickly. Change, obviously, has always been an integral part of business life. Some organizations, however, seem to cope with change better than others. In the future, the ability to handle change successfully will become even more vital. As we see it, several major areas of change will have a profound effect on business in the future, and the executives who will be able to lead their organizations through these changes will be the ones to survive and prosper.

GLOBAL MARKETS, MULTIPLE CULTURES

The first type of change that is accelerating is globalization. Although this phenomenon has been discussed before, there are some characteristics of globalization that are not always understood. First, barriers to trade are coming down all over the world. Europe has set 1992 as a target date to finally become a common market. The United States and Europe are exerting great pressure on Japan to open its borders and are starting to succeed. I am convinced that not a single person could have predicted the extent or the rapidity of the changes that occurred in 1989 across Eastern Europe or, for that matter, those that are currently taking place in the Soviet Union, which, along with China, will become a more important trading partner of the West. The consequence of this trend is that companies can no longer plan without considering the world as the marketplace. The recent fight for Firestone by Bridgestone of Japan, Pirrelli of Italy, and Michelin of France is a good example. The fact that the automobile market has become global is forcing the tire manufacturers to themselves become international competitors. Cummins Engine Company, which dominated the U.S. market for many years, suddenly found itself surrounded by new competitors in the 1980s. The competition first came from Europe—Volvo and Mercedes Benz—and then from the Japanese manufacturers Komatsu and Hino.

Even a very successful midsize client of ours in the Northeast, which has carved out a very comfortable niche for itself in the chemical industry, suddenly found one morning that a new Japanese competitor was establishing a plant only a few hundred yards up the road.

The consequence of this internationalization of business is the impact it will have on corporate planning. Decisions affecting product design, manufacturing sites, marketing approaches, distribution systems, and customer service will vary greatly from one market to another. The reason is simple. Although the marketplace will be global in scope, it is not now, nor will it be, homogeneous in character. In Europe, language and culture differ in each country. Customs and traditions vary greatly from one Asian nation to the next. Even the United States is becoming multicultural with the advent of the Hispanic, Korean, Japanese, Filipino, and Vietnamese immigrants—to name but a few groups that are changing the fabric of the country more than in any immigration wave of the past.

Sir John Harvey-Jones, the former chairman of ICI (Imperial Chemical Industries), explained the phenomenon well at a meeting of the American Chamber of Commerce in London. "The cliché that the world is a single market is, in reality, not true. Each market requires different responses and it is the ability to read that response and apply that response which will be the key." This will require companies to be global in perspective but culturally sensitive on a market-to-market basis. Gary DiCamillo of Black & Decker recently told *The Journal of Business Strategy* (Nov./ Dec. 1989) how his company is trying to cope with this phenomenon.

As you go around the world, many power tools are used in similar ways so that there need not be major differences in the products. . . . We don't need to reinvent the power tool in every country, but rather, we have a common product and adapt it to individual markets. The products are marketed quite differently in some cases due to local customs.

"THINK GLOBAL, ACT LOCAL"

Historically, U.S. companies have not been very adept at dealing across geographic or cultural boundaries. Japanese, Dutch, West German, and Swedish companies have shown greater versatility in dealing with a multicultural business world. Sony, for example, made a different Walkman for Norway than it did for Sweden even though these were two of its smallest markets. American executives have not traveled or lived abroad as much as executives from these other countries. Japan's companies sent hundreds of thousands of their executives to study and live in the United States in order to master English, U.S. customs, and American culture several years before they set about to conquer U.S. markets.

One of our long-term clients, 3M, has been a rare exception to the U.S. experience. At 3M there is a slogan that permeates all the foreign subsidiaries: "Think global, act local." This will be a fundamental rule of success in the future. Companies will have to act locally in a marketing and selling sense in order to flush out the distinctive needs of each market but globally on a manufacturing, distribution, and customer service basis in order to achieve the required levels of critical mass for costs and value.

The need for executives to become "global strategists: working as deftly in Tokyo as in Toledo," as *U.S. News & World Report* (March 7, 1988) suggested, will accelerate in the twenty-first century. American business will have to learn global strategies and tactics in order to compete successfully. Overseas corporations are more skillful at developing strategies for foreign markets because they have been doing business outside their own countries for centuries and can better navigate unfamiliar terrain. U.S. business is not being assisted by U.S. business schools which, for the most part, teach techniques based on concepts that apply primarily to the domestic market and, therefore, are parochial and outdated in today's global marketplace.

MORE COMPETITORS AND MORE INTENSE COMPETITION

The next trend that will become accentuated in the twenty-first century will be that of competition. There will be more competitors, causing more intense competition. As barriers to competition go down, more and more companies will see the world as their market and will want to jump into the game. The U.S. auto market used to belong to the "Big Three"— General Motors, Ford, and Chrysler. With the coming of Toyota, Nissan, Honda, and Subaru, that is no longer true. Hyundai, from Korea, has also entered the game. One must remember, however, that there are thirteen car manufacturers in Japan, and Malaysia has just set up a car assembly plant. Each of these manufacturers will have to play the global marketplace in order to survive in its domestic market. This will bring not only more competitors but also more severe competition. Corporate managements will require finely tuned competitive skills in order to prosper into the twenty-first century.

The same trend is occurring in the financial markets. With the advent of the "big bang" day in London in the summer of 1987, their world has not been the same. Financial service companies that had never heard of each other suddenly became bitter rivals. The playing field has also changed dramatically in the health care and airline industries because of deregulation. This process, which started in the United States, is beginning to spread abroad, with Europe now considering a similar policy.

SCARCER HUMAN RESOURCES

Employees will be a scarce resource for American companies in the next century. One reason is due to the downsizing of these companies in the 1980s. Downsizing may have made these organizations "lean and mean," but at the same time, early retirement programs have deprived them of valuable experience and talent. Fewer, and younger, people will now be required to make more important decisions than they ever had to before.

Furthermore, the current phenomenon of the "aging of America," whereby it is forecast that 60 percent of the population will be older than 55 by the year 2000, will result in no replacement pool of younger people to take the retirees' place. Corporations will have to find ways to substantially improve productivity without adding employees. They will also have to teach people how to make effective decisions without the benefit of experience. The Japanese have already solved the first problem. Japan's automobile industry produces the same number of cars as its U.S. counterpart, but with 700,000 fewer people.

Some skills will be in short supply. Engineers, in particular, will be a sought-after group. The number of engineers being graduated in U.S. schools is far less than in Japan and West Germany, and is also far less than what America requires.

BETTER QUALITY

The Japanese started the trend for better quality. By bringing in Dr. Deming and Dr. Juran to teach their people better techniques of quality control and thus improve the performance and reliability of their products, they have now made quality improvements the standard operating procedure worldwide. Because of the enormous strides made by the Japanese and seen by consumers around the world, quality is again perceived as a desirable element for which consumers are willing to pay. Unfortunately, the West Germans and the Japanese lead the world in quality, and because of the years it will take to obtain even marginal improvement, the

United States is far behind and trying to catch up. Nine years after having caught the "quality" bug, U.S. car manufacturers have had a 25 percent to 40 percent improvement in quality. However, U.S. cars still have 88.6 defects per 100 cars versus 47.3 defects per 100 cars for the Japanese. This gap will take years, if not decades, to close.

Most U.S. companies that were faced with the "Japanese challenge" in the 1970s reacted in the wrong way. Most accused the Japanese of exploiting cheap labor and gaining market share by underpricing U.S. companies with lower priced, "me-too" products. Unfortunately, that was not the case. One company, when presented with this challenge, saw it differently. Cummins Engine, in a February 1988 *Management Review* article, explained, "In our view, share gain by the competition [Japanese] was mostly won fair and square, with better products, better quality, better prices, and better responsiveness to the customer."

Instead of crying to the government for protection against these firms, Cummins set about to help itself by redoubling its efforts in three areas: product price, cost, and performance. Cummins also taught its employees to remove the word "foreign" before "competition" and replace it with the word "international." This took the emotion out of the issue and encouraged people to address the problem rationally. As a result, Cummins has not lost a single point of its domestic market share (in fact it has grown), and it has increased its international sales dramatically.

GM, Ford, and Chrysler have not found a way to sell their cars in Japan, yet the Japanese cannot get enough Volkswagens, Mercedes, Volvos, and BMWs. The difference, in our opinion, derives from the same reason why these products attract U.S. customers—better quality.

INNOVATION

3M has a standard by which it measures the performance of all its business units. Twenty-five percent of each unit's sales must come from products that did not exist five years before. This criteria has caused 3M to introduce some two hundred new products each year and has given it a reputation as one of America's most innovative companies. Unfortunately, the same cannot be said for most industries in the United States. In general, U.S. companies are losing their innovative edge. A February 1988 article in *The Academy of Management Executive* makes this point quite clearly:

Many market losses experienced by American firms can be attributed to a *lack* of *emphasis* on *product* and *process innovation*. *Product innovations* create new market opportunities, and in many industries are the driving force behind growth and profitability. *Process innovations* enable firms to produce existing products more efficiently. As such, process innovations are one of the main determinants of productivity growth. In this technologically dynamic era, without a continual stream of product and process innovations, firms soon lose their ability to compete effectively.

The authors—Charles Hill, Michael Hitt, and Robert Hoskisson—went on to point out that America's declining competitiveness is due to a decrease over the last five years in both product and process innovation compared to other countries such as Japan, West Germany, Italy, and even the United Kingdom. They attributed the cause of this decline to the "quantitative" management systems espoused in the United States such as "ROI [return on investment]-based financial controls and portfolio management concepts." These principles, they argued, "give rise to a short-term orientation and risk avoidance. . . . The argument to this point has been that reliance on tight financial controls by the corporate office encourages decision-making at the divisional level consistent with short-run profit maximization and risk avoidance. The result is lower innovative activity and declining competitiveness."

The risk-avoidance style of management in existence today in many U.S. companies has already cost the country dearly. Many inventions that were birthed in America have seen the light of day as innovative new products abroad. One example is the transistor, which was invented by Bell Laboratories but exploited by Sony of Japan. A second is the videocassette, which was invented by California-based Ampex but exploited by Sony and JVC.

The Japanese, on the other hand, are spending more on research and development (R & D) and taking more risks than their U.S. counterparts. In 1986, for example, Japanese companies outspent U.S. companies by $72 billion to $59 billion. While Japan is becoming more innovative, the United States seems to be losing its innovative spirit.

Another signal of that trend can be seen in the number of patents issued in the last few years. General Electric, the powerhouse of American innovation, had been number one in terms of number of patents issued to a company for twenty-five straight years until 1986. In 1987, General Electric tumbled to fourth place, surpassed by three Japanese companies—Canon, Hitachi, and Toshiba. The Japanese registered a total of 17,288 patents in 1987, an increase of 25 percent over the previous year. Canon has had a remarkable record, pushing its annual number of patents from 158 to 887. During the same time, General Electric's patents fell from 822 to 784. Even the West Germans and the French are increasing, annually, their patent registration by 15 percent and 19 percent respectively, while the U.S. share is decreasing. It is no wonder that these astute and technically oriented Japanese companies have taken over the market for such items as copiers and cameras. "America's technological leadership is slipping," *Time* magazine recently noted (March 21, 1988). In order to survive the next century, U.S. business will have to rekindle its technical prowess.

This trend will probably continue. The latest quantitative game in town is "shareholder value." This system encourages chief executive officers (CEOs) to judge businesses on their ability to enhance or reduce value for the shareholders. It also encourages CEOs to trade businesses on this criterion alone. This is strategic folly. This "numbers approach" can kill innovation. Even when employees can come up with a good new product concept, management may not have the nerve to pursue it. A good example is the videocassette technology that was developed by Ampex in the United States but exploited by Sony and JVC in Japan.

On the other hand, we have had the opportunity to work with many fast-growing midsized companies that are run by their original founders, and we have noted that these people know only too well that continuous profits are best generated by a steady stream of new products. Because of the focus on numbers, however, we see a growing need for better strategic management of large corporations. A management approach based more on the assessment of the qualitative variables facing industry, together with a desire to rejuvenate the innovative juices of corporate America, are sorely needed.

INFORMATION EXPLOSION

Another trend that will exacerbate industry challenges in the next decades is the increase in the amount of information to which executives will have access when making decisions. IBM estimates that with the advent of personal computers (PCs), super-computers, and on-line databases, managers will have seven to ten times more information available to make decisions in the year 2000 than they have today. There is no doubt that more accurate information contributes to better decision making. It is also true that too much information can paralyze decision making. Waiting for more, or perfect, information can delay a decision and cause the decision maker to "miss the boat." In the twenty-first century, people will require more acute skills and thinking processes to be able to separate relevant from irrelevant information more quickly and thus make better and more timely decisions. There will also be less room for error since most wrong decisions will have greater and more far-reaching negative consequences. A minor decision gone wrong may have repercussions around the globe.

SUMMARY

What do these trends mean for corporations everywhere as they head into the twenty-first century? In our view, the twenty-first century will require strong leadership. It will be very good for people and organizations that develop and practice leadership skills. Proactive leadership will require the ability to detect, assess, and exploit these trends to an organization's greatest benefit. Leadership, however, is an elusive word which has different meanings to different people. To us, leadership has a very specific meaning and requires the mastery of very discrete and deliberate skills and management processes, which we will explore in the remainder of this book.

2

What Is Leadership?

"Follow me," Lawrence of Arabia shouted to his Arab troops as he led his army's charge into battle.

Although the term "leadership" is frequently used, few executives in business today can be considered true leaders. The ultimate test of a leader is whether he or she will be followed as Lawrence of Arabia was followed by an army of people who were not of his race or religion. For the followers to allow themselves to be led assumes their implicit belief in the leader's ability.

Many books have been written on leadership, but few have been able to describe it in comprehensible terms, nor have they been able to describe the skills of leadership in any detail except to attribute it to a "trait of personality." John P. Kotter, in his 1988 book called *The Leadership Factor,* explains that leadership can be defined, analyzed, and learned. He also pointed out that it is not taught in business schools. Unfortunately, he did not articulate how leadership can be attained. Jack Welch, the CEO of General Electric, views it this way:

A leader is someone who can develop a vision of what he or she wants their business, their unit, their activity to do and be. Somebody who is able to articulate to the entire unit what the unit is and gain through a sharing of the discussion—listening and talking—an acceptance of that vision. And then can relentlessly drive implementation of that vision to a successful conclusion. (*Business Weekly,* December 14, 1987)

This definition of leadership is probably as close a definition as we could conjure up ourselves. However, hidden in the above statement are the mention of three very different sets of skills and critical thinking processes.

Our view is that there are some fundamental skills of leadership that can be articulated, learned, and perfected by almost anyone in any organization. Leadership consists of mastering three critical processes of management that should be practiced consciously.

THREE FUNDAMENTAL SKILLS OF LEADERSHIP

There are, in our view, three fundamental skills of leadership. Without these, the leader will not be followed. Unfortunately, none of these skills are taught in the formal education system, business schools, or any corporation's management development program. Most leaders who have acquired these skills have done so by experience, by osmosis (intuitively), or by experience on the "firing line." However, these skills can also be acquired in a conscious and deliberate manner.

The first skill is *strategic thinking*. It is the thought process used by a leader to formulate, articulate, and communicate a coherent strategy and vision for the organization. Followers want to know where they are being led. General Motors's CEO, Roger Smith, in a *Fortune* article, said that the only thing he would do differently if he started his term as CEO over again would be to communicate his vision of General Motors (GM) earlier and more frequently than he did. He cited this failure as the major reason for his inability to turn GM around more quickly (February 13, 1989).

The second skill is *innovative thinking*. Companies need to constantly find new opportunities in order to grow. A leader must be able to initiate, promote, and develop in others these special abilities. In order to do so, he or she must understand the process of innovation and be able to instill it in every member of the organization.

The third skill is the ability to deal with operational *problems* and *decisions* successfully. This is a three-part process that we call rational decision making. Again, this must be part of the fabric of an organization so that issues can be addressed both incisively and decisively.

STRATEGIC THINKING

Strategic thinking is the process used by a leader to formulate, articulate, communicate, and implement a clear, concise, and explicit strategy and vision for the organization. Unfortunately, in many organizations the strategy of the company is not always clear. It usually resides in the head of the chief executive officer exclusively. Other people around the CEO have to guess at the strategy. Because they have not been involved in the process, or because the CEO cannot clearly articulate the strategy, they feel no commitment to, or ownership of, that vision. Our own experience with some 250 organizations of all sizes and in various industries around the world has shown that most managers are so engrossed in operational activity that they have not developed the skills to think strategically. A CEO, therefore, might wish to involve his or her subordinates in a deliberate strategic process strictly for its educational value. The problem, however, is that most CEOs practice this process by osmosis and are not conscious of its various steps. It is usually impossible to transfer to anyone else a skill that one cannot describe. The strategic thinking process has the following broad steps.

Assess the Environment

Any sound strategy must allow the organization to successfully deal with its environment. Thus, the first step in strategic thinking is an assessment of the qualitative variables that will be working for or against the business in the future. These variables, however, usually have been considered only by the management team and must be extracted and debated in a structured and objective forum with an outside person facilitating the process. The qualitative variables are usually highly subjective in nature and consist of each person's view of what may or may not occur inside and, more important, outside the organization. These differing views must be discussed in a rational manner in order to agree on the most important factors that the business will have to face.

Determine the Business's Strategic Heartbeat

The next step is for the management team to identify which component of the business is strategically most important to the organization's survival and serves as the key determinant of the company's products, markets, and customers. In other words, which part of the business is at the root of the organization and can be leveraged by the company as its strategic weapon against its environment? This concept is known as the driving force, and will be discussed in more detail in the next chapter.

Develop a Coherent Strategy and Business Concept

Around the key determinant, which will drive the organization forward, it is now imperative to develop a statement of strategy that can be communicated to the individuals who will be called on to carry it out. It needs to be articulated in terms precise and concise enough so that people can carry it around in their heads. The statement should represent the conceptual underpinning of the organization and its raison d'être.

Translate the Strategy into a Strategic Profile and Vision

The next step is to translate the strategy into a vision of what the business will look like sometime in the future. This vision should be a description of the products, customers, market segments, and geographic markets that the organization will emphasize and deemphasize in the future. This vision or profile then serves everyone as a "test bed" (or description) for the allocation of resources and the types of opportunities that are to be pursued in the future.

Anticipate the Implications of Your Strategy

Frequently a good strategy can go astray because management did not think through its implications. The next step, then, is to test the strategy in a variety of ways to flush out its implications and identify the critical issues that will need to be addressed in order to make the strategy work. Too often these implications are not considered and management finds itself reacting to them after the fact instead of having anticipated them in advance and dealing with them proactively. These critical issues can then be assigned to specific people who have the responsibility to manage them to a successful resolution. Monitoring the progress being made on these issues and drawing these issues to a conclusion will assure the success of the strategy and vision.

INNOVATIVE THINKING

The second fundamental skill of leadership is the ability to innovate and, in particular, to promote this kind of thinking in others. Generating concepts for new and better products, new customers, and new markets, and also for ways to improve the way in which the business is run, are key to an organization's survival. The best companies today appear driven to continuously innovate. Some organizations, however, have shown more skill at it than others. In our view, it is because these organizations have mastered the *process* of innovation. The key trait of leaders, is to master this skill themselves and to aid subordinates in its gestation.

When we first started to look into the subject of innovation by going to our clients and observing them trying to innovate, we seemed to be entering a world of sorcery. When we asked innovative people what they or their organizations felt was the origin of their skill, they gave answers such as "accidents," "flashes of genius," or "lightning bolts out of the blue." However, when we watched these people while they worked, we found no accidents. Instead, what we observed was the practice of a very systematic, deliberate, and discrete process at work, being used by osmosis, but nevertheless being used. The process that we saw has four steps.

Search the Environment for Opportunities

The most fundamental concept of innovation is that change is the raw material and fuel of innovation. There can be no innovation without change. Change creates turmoil, and out of turmoil comes opportunity. The more change, the more opportunity; the less change, the less opportunity.

Therefore, innovative people and organizations see change as healthy and as a consistent source of opportunity. The best innovators, however, do not wait for change to find them. They seem to know exactly where, in the environment, to search for changes that can be transformed into good business opportunities. There are ten such environmental sources which will be explored in more detail in the following chapters.

Assess and Rank the Opportunities

Not all opportunities should be pursued. There are bad, good, and excellent opportunities. Therefore, the opportunities that are found need to be ranked in terms of their potential benefit to the organization. There are four important criteria to consider in this step, which will be discussed in chapter 4. From this assessment, the best opportunities, like cream, will start rising to the top of the list.

Develop the Critical Factors for Success or Failure

The fact that an opportunity ends up at the top of the list is no guarantee that it can be pursued successfully. The third step of innovation, then, is to identify the potential best case and worst case outcomes that each opportunity could bring to the organization. This is important for two reasons. One, we can now discuss the risk/reward relationship of each opportunity and further reduce our list to the crème de la crème of the opportunities available. Second, we can now identify the critical factors that will cause the best case or worst case scenarios to occur.

Construct a Plan to Pursue the Best Opportunities

Some people think that good innovators are not good implementors. This is not the case. The best innovators we saw could conceptualize as well as implement their innovations successfully. They did this by anticipating actions that could prevent the negative critical factors from happening and bringing about the worst case outcomes, and by anticipating actions to promote the critical factors that would bring about the best case scenario. These actions would then be made part and parcel of a step-by-step implementation plan to carry out each opportunity. Each step would be assigned to an "owner" for execution, together with target dates for completion and review dates to monitor progress.

As Henry Adams said in 1907: "Chaos often breeds life, when order breeds habit." Although the environment and changes seem to behave in a chaotic manner, a systematic process of innovation can breed a habit that can help people and leaders deal with chaos successfully.

DECISION MAKING

While a leader is thinking strategically in order to best position his or her organization in relation to its environment and is encouraging innovation to identify new opportunities, he or she must also deal effectively with the operational issues that surface each day. Although people seem to be bombarded by a variety of different issues from the time they arrive at work until the time they leave, there are only three types of issues that people face each day; however, they do so over and over again. The three types are problems, decisions, and decisions or plans to be implemented. Each of these can be resolved through the application of rational thinking, creative thinking, or both.

Rational thinking has three processes. The first is Problem Analysis. This process is used when we are faced with a situation in which something has gone wrong and no one knows what caused such an event to occur. Problem Analysis is a process used to logically diagnose a problem in order to identify its root cause and bring about corrective action.

Decision Analysis, on the other hand, is a process used when we are faced with having to make a choice among several options or alternatives, all of which seem to be good, and when the best alternative is not evident. Decision Analysis can help us methodically sort our way through the alternatives in order to identify the best one.

Once a tentative decision has been made, however, it must be implemented successfully, and thus the third rational process, Potential Problem Analysis, comes into play. A detailed implementation plan is drawn up and then explored for potential problems. By anticipating what might go wrong with the plan, we can also anticipate actions to prevent these potential problems from happening or, at least, have contingent actions ready to minimize their effect should they occur. The original plan is then modified to include the best preventive and contingent actions we have generated, and the modified plan is the one we pursue since it has a better chance of working than the original one.

SUMMARY

These three processes—strategic thinking, innovation, and decision making—are the fundamental processes that leaders must master in order to demonstrate leadership qualities. They must also be able to instill these skills in their followers.

- *Strategic thinking* provides the visionary leader with the tool to articulate his or her vision and to motivate other people to adopt it as their own. Usually people can more easily implement something that they understand and feel ownership of.
- The *process of innovation* provides the leader with a tool to promote the notion of continuous improvement, which is a must for any organization that intends to survive. Our process, however, demystifies innovation and puts it into terms that can make it a repeatable business practice.
- The *process of decision making* is a key skill to master in order to deal effectively with the day-to-day issues that arise. These issues are somewhat operational in nature, but we cannot go forward without dealing with today's concerns, crises, problems, and decisions.

The best leaders, in fact, are those who can pass on, or teach, their skills to others. We cannot do this until we are fully conscious of the process or methods we use to achieve success. Good athletes usually do not make good coaches because while they were athletes they never analyzed the process or method that they were practicing and that made them successful. As a result, when they become coaches, athletes cannot develop these skills in anyone else because they cannot describe these skills. The best coaches, on the other hand, were not necessarily the best athletes but were, rather, "students of the game." These are the people who studied the methods or processes used by successful athletes; they discovered them and now can pass them on to others. A casual jogger does not necessarily pay much attention to the mechanics of jogging. However, if the jogger wishes to compete successfully in a marathon, he or she needs to become familiar with the technique, or *process,* of running in order to run in the most effective manner.

The same is true of leadership. The process of leadership can be studied and learned. We studied leaders in many organizations, and the processes described briefly above were the ones that these people had mastered. The following chapters will explore each of these processes in more depth. A good leader will need to develop the conscious use of these processes in his or her subordinates in order to lead effectively. The reason is simple: It is a lot easier to lead a well-trained army than a bunch of ragamuffins. As John Kotter pointed out in *The Leadership Factor,* during peacetime, an army needs few leaders, but during a time of war, it needs many. The same is true during a time of commercial warfare. The more leaders you have in your organization, the higher the probability of winning.

A conscious management process can then be institutionalized as a repeatable business practice. In other words, over time the process can become a reflex. The notion of cascading these processes down the organization is also critical to the success of a leader. The reason is simple. Unlike what many think, a leader in business is not only a leader of people but also a manager of processes. It is the processes that the leader puts into place in the organization that will get people to behave in a certain manner. The dissemination of these three fundamental processes throughout the organization is then vital to its success. The winning organization, in the long run, is not the one that can out-muscle its competitors with technical skills but rather the one that can out-think its opponents. Unfortunately, thinking is a rare skill in American business today. The best leaders have mastered the skills of critical thinking and have the ability to instill these skills in the dozens, hundreds, or even thousands of people around them.

3

The Leader as Strategist

Our firm has been involved in the area of strategy since the mid-1970s. Back then there was an explosion of literature on the subject of strategy and we started browsing through these books to try to get an understanding of what strategy meant. Unfortunately, we became more confused than enlightened. The reason was simple. Each person who wrote about strategy used the word with a different meaning. Some authors said that "strategy" was the goal or objective, and tactics were the means. Others gave the word "strategy" a completely different meaning. They said that the objective was the goal and that the strategy was the means. These two definitions are 180 degrees apart in meaning.

The second element we noticed about these books was that most of them were written by professors in business schools who had never even talked to the companies about which they were writing. In fact, their formulas were developed by trying to *recreate* the "magic recipe" that a particular company had followed to become successful. Our approach was different. We said to ourselves: "Let's go out and talk to people who actually run organizations. And let's find out what strategy means to them." We went out and started interviewing CEOs in a variety of different industries and in different sized companies. Eventually, we participated in the sessions these CEOs had with their key people while they were wrestling with the issue of strategy. What you will find in this chapter are the concepts and key ideas that we heard these people discussing and debating. The process described in the remainder of this chapter is a reflection of the thought patterns that we saw effective CEOs use.

THE STRATEGIC THINKING PROCESS

The first observation we made, while sitting in on these sessions, was that every person who ran a company had a "vision" of what he or she wanted that company to look like at some point in the future. Basically, they employed and deployed the assets and resources of their organization in pursuit of that vision. Graphically, it would look like this:

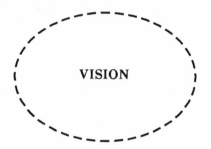

Strategic thinking, then, is the type of thinking that occurs inside the head of the CEO and his or her key executives and that attempts to clarify and articulate this vision. Strategic thinking then translates the vision into a profile of what they want the organization to become.

```
STRATEGIC
PROFILE
```

This profile or vision becomes the target for all corporate decisions and plans. The decisions and plans that are pursued are those that fall within the parameters of the vision or profile, and the decisions or plans that are not pursued are those that fall outside those boundaries.

Another way to look at this concept is to separate the activities of any executive team into "what" and "how." These two activities go on inside any organization. In other words, some of the thinking conducted in a company will determine what it will become as an organization, while other types of thinking determine "how" it will get there. Another observation that we made during these sessions with management teams was that although both types of thinking went on in any organization, they went on with different levels of proficiency. Some corporations were proficient at both. In other words, management had a well-articulated strategy, which was well communicated and understood; in addition, on a day-to-day basis, they were very good managers of the business. They were proficient at both the "what" and the "how."

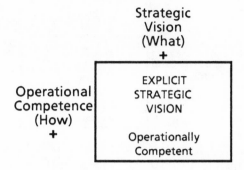

Other firms that we observed had been very good managers of the business operationally, sometimes for long periods of time, but did not always know where the business was headed. They could not describe what the business would look like sometime in the future.

Still other firms knew exactly what they were trying to become, but their difficulty lay in making it happen (how).

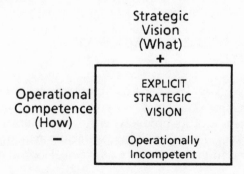

Finally, we also found the worst of both worlds, firms that did not know what they were trying to become nor how to get there.

Let us now place all four quadrants on a matrix and give you an assignment: In which quadrant would you place your organization?

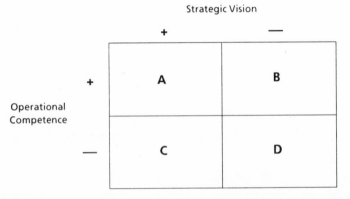

If you chose quadrant B, you have placed yourself with 80 percent of the firms with whom we work, and you can consider yourself normal. The reason for this is simple. Most firms are so involved in operational activity that they do not spend enough time thinking about the future of the business. The remainder of this chapter will outline some of the key concepts of strategic thinking.

DETERMINE THE FUTURE STRATEGIC PROFILE OF THE BUSINESS

How do we go about describing the future profile for an organization? The answer is simple. The "look" or profile of an organization is determined by the nature of its products, customers, market segments, and geographic markets. Therefore, if management wants to guide the direction of the organization and influence its eventual look, it must determine, in advance, which products, customers, market segments, and geographic markets it will pursue, as well as which products, customers, market segments, and geographic markets it will not pursue.

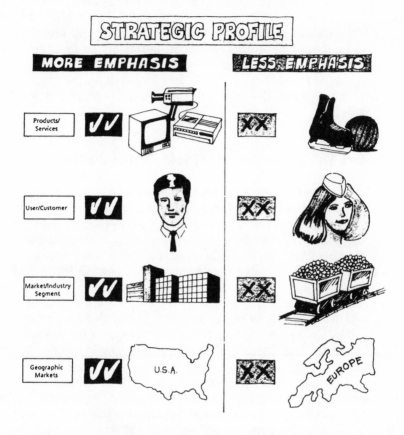

Strategically, it is more important to know to what the strategy or vision does not lend itself than it is to know to what it does. The reason for this is that management personnel perform two critical tasks that set the direction of the organization and influence its eventual look. First, they allocate resources. Allocating resources strategically means giving more resources to the areas of the future strategic profile that the company wants to emphasize. In other words, activities that will bring in products, customers, market segments, and geographic markets that resemble items on the left side of our profile will get preferential treatment. Activities that will bring items that resemble those on the right side of our profile will not get resources.

The second most important strategic task of management is to identify which opportunities the organization should be pursuing. The future strategic profile is again the final filter for these. Opportunities that will bring the firm items that resemble the ones on the left side will receive preferential treatment over those that do not. With a profile or vision articulated in this manner and imbedded in the heads of all the key people in the organization, we can now start to manage strategically. This profile or vision becomes the ultimate test bed for all decisions made in the organization.

The next question that comes to mind is, how do we go about determining the line of demarcation between the items that will receive more emphasis and those that will receive less emphasis in the future? The answer to this question gives rise to the most important concept of strategic thinking.

DETERMINE THE STRATEGIC HEARTBEAT OF THE BUSINESS

The true test to determine whether an organization has a strategy is to watch management when it is faced with the decision of whether to pursue a certain opportunity. During such discussions we noted that although management used a hierarchy of different filters, the ultimate filter was always whether there was a fit between the products, customers, and markets that the opportunity brought and one key component of the business. In other words, one part of the business seemed to be strategically more important to managers than all others. If they found a good fit there, they would more than likely pursue that opportunity; if they did not find a good fit, they would not. However, the one element of the business that seemed to be the final filter varied from one company to another. In each company, then, there seemed to be something that was at the root of that company's existence and was pushing, propelling, or driving it forward. One component of the business seemed to dominate management thinking. This was its strategic heartbeat and the *driving force* of the business.

When exploring this concept further, we found that there are basically ten components to any business. These are:

1. Product/Service Concept,
2. Market Type/Category,
3. User/Customer Class,
4. Production Capacity/Capability,
5. Technology/Know-How,
6. Sales/Marketing Method,
7. Distribution Method,
8. Natural Resources,
9. Size/Growth, and
10. Return/Profit

For management to clearly understand what strategic area of the business is driving the business and serves as its heartbeat is fundamental to that management team's ability to make intelligent choices about future products, customers, market segments, and geographic markets. Failure to understand this key concept is what leads to strategic ineffectiveness.

DEFINITIONS OF DRIVING FORCE

Product-Driven Company

A product-driven company is one that is "locked" into a product *concept* of some kind whose function and look do not change much over time. Future products are adaptations, modifications, or extensions of the current product. In other words, future product offerings emanating from such a company are derivatives of the existing product, and the existing product is a "genetic" derivative of the original product.

The automobile industry, in general, is a good example. The look and function of the automobile has not changed for a hundred years, and probably will not change for the next hundred. GM, Ford, Toyota, and Chrysler are all pursuing a product-driven strategy. Other companies following such a concept are Boeing, with its concept of a "flying machine"; insurance companies, with "insurance" as a concept; and heavy equipment manufacturers, who keep making derivatives of their existing machines. IBM is locked into the concept of "computing machines," and, as such, computers of various sizes is what it produces.

Market Category–Driven Company

This company is very different from the product-driven firm. A market-driven company is one that has deliberately anchored its business to a describable category of market. That market, then, is the only one it serves. The firm's strategy is to continuously scrutinize that market in an attempt to identify related needs. Once these needs are found, then appropriate products, which may otherwise be unrelated to each other, are made.

One example is American Hospital Supply. In its very name, this company has identified the market to which its business is anchored—the hospital. The strategy of the company is to respond to a variety of needs coming from that market. As a result, the product scope of such a firm ranges from bedpans to sutures and from gauze pads to electronic imaging systems. These products are unrelated to each other—not genetic derivatives. The only common thread is that they are all used in a hospital.

User Class–Driven Company

This company's strategy is similar to a market category–driven firm except that this company has anchored its business to a discrete *class* of end users. Johnson & Johnson's strategy of making products for "doctors, nurses, patients and mothers" is a good example.

Production Capacity/Capability–Driven Company

A capacity-driven strategy is usually pursued by a company that has a substantial investment in its production facility, and the thrust is to keep that facility operating at maximum capacity. The drive is to look for opportunities that can utilize whatever the production capacity can handle. Paper companies, because of enormous capital tied up in their mills, are examples of organizations that usually pursue a capacity-driven strategy. These companies will get into newsprint, fine paper, toilet tissue, disposable diapers, paper towels, and other products in order to optimize their production capacity. A production capability–driven company is one that has built some unique capabilities into its production process and pursues only opportunities that can utilize these unique capabilities. Specialized printers are good examples.

Technology/Know-How–Driven Company

This company is one that has the ability to invent or acquire hard or soft technology or know-how. Then it goes out looking for applications of that technology or know-how. Over time such a company gets involved in a broad array of products, all of which stem from the particular technology, and serves a broad array of customers and market segments. Dupont and 3M are good examples of such companies.

Sales/Marketing Method–Driven Company

This company has a unique way of attracting orders from its customers. Such a company will only offer products and pursue customers that can be brought together through that selling method. Door-to-door companies such as Mary Kay, Tupperware, and Electrolux are good examples. Catalogue companies are another. Any product that can be advertised in the catalogue will be considered.

Distribution Method–Driven Company

This company pursues a strategy that is the opposite of that of a sales/marketing method–driven firm. This company has in place a unique distribution method to get products to the customers. All products or services offered must utilize that distribution method or else will not be offered. Telephone operating companies, with their vast networks, are good examples of such companies. Department stores are another. Sears Roebuck, with its 850 stores across the United States, will push through any product to any customers that they can match with it, from furniture to financial services.

Natural Resources—Driven Company

When pursuit of, or access to, natural resources becomes the strategic drive of an organization, such a company can be perceived as pursuing a resource-driven strategy. Energy companies are examples of such organizations. Exxon, Newmont Mining, and Consolidated Goldfields are such companies.

Size/Growth—Driven Company

A company whose only criteria for getting in or out of business is an appetite for size and growth is one that is motivated by this driving force. Conglomerates that pursue growth for the sake of growth, as W. R. Grace did for many years, are good examples.

Return/Profit—Driven Company

When profit becomes the only criteria for getting in or out of businesses, then such a company is allowing this driving force to dominate its strategy. ITT, under Geneen, was a good example.

At this point, we would like to give you another assignment.

- Which driving force mentioned above is currently acting as the heartbeat of your business and driving your strategy?
- Which driving force do you think each of your key subordinates would *say* drives your company and acts as the strategic heartbeat of the business?

Our experience shows that when we pose these questions to a management team, there will be as many responses as there are people in the room at the time. Different people have different views as to what area of the business is propelling it forward and is the key determinant of the company's products, customers, and markets. Unfortunately, if there is lack of consensus and clarity around this key concept, the organization will zigzag its way forward.

Another set of key questions to pose once management has agreed (and getting agreement is not an easy task) about what is currently driving the business are these:

p45,6 46

- What should drive the business in the future?
- Should we continue to be driven as we have been or should we explore another driving force?
- If we explore a new driving force, which one should that be?
- What implications will that have on the choices that we make on the nature of products, customers, and markets that we do or do not offer?
- What will we end up looking like as an organization if we change the driving force of our company?

ARTICULATE THE BUSINESS CONCEPT

The driving force concept is a tool to allow management to identify which area of the business is at the root of its company's products, customers, and markets, and is strategically more important to that company than any other area.

However, it is also a tool to allow management to articulate its concept of doing business in that mode. Every business is founded on a concept of some kind. We now need to formulate a one-paragraph statement that explains how this component is the heartbeat of the business and how it will propel or drive the organization and dictate its behavior in the choice of future products, markets, and customers. This statement will be the conceptual underpinning of the business.

Depending on which driving force is chosen, the organization's business concept or strategy will be dramatically different. Even when different companies have the same driving force, they may still have business concepts different enough from each other to be going in different directions. Some good examples are found in the automobile industry: Volvo, BMW, Mercedes, Volkswagen, and General Motors can all be said to be product-driven: they produce only automobiles. However, each of these companies has a very different conception of its product.

Volvo makes "safe and durable cars."

Mercedes makes the "best engineered car."

BMW makes "the ultimate driving machine."

Volkswagen makes the "people's car."

General Motors makes "a car for each income strata."

As a result, each of these companies goes down a slightly different road and seldom competes with each other even though they all make a similar product—a car.

KEEP THE STRATEGY STRONG AND HEALTHY

As we observed companies over the years, we noted that there were some that could perpetuate their strategy successfully over long periods of time, like IBM or Daimler-Benz. Others, however, had great difficulty doing that, and their performance level over time resembled that of a yo-yo. What, we asked, was the difference?

Over time, the strategy of an organization can, like a person, get stronger and healthier or weak and ill. What determines, in our opinion, which way it will go are the areas of excellence that a company deliberately cultivates over time to keep the strategy strong and healthy and to give it an edge in the marketplace. An area of excellence, another key concept of strategic thinking, is a describable skill or capability that a company has cultivated to a level of proficiency greater than anything else it does, and, particularly, better than anyone else does. It is excellence in these two or three key areas that keeps the strategy alive and working. Bill Marriott, of the Marriott hotel chain, said, "It took the company over a decade to figure out that it had special expertise in running hospitality and food-service operations." This "special expertise" or capability is what we call an area of excellence. One could also call it a strategic skill.

The concept of identifying the areas of excellence that the company needs to cultivate to make its strategy succeed is critical because they vary greatly from one driving force to another. If a company is product-driven, for its strategy to work it must have the best product on the market. Therefore, it must excel at two key skills: One is *product development* and the second is *product servicing*. Of all the things this company needs to do well, it must perform these two tasks better than well, and better than any competitor, since the name of the game is "best product wins!"

A user class–driven company, on the other hand, must excel at very different skills. Because it has anchored its business around a class of user, and only that class, it must know that user class better than anyone else does if its strategy is to succeed because it services only one user. Therefore, *user research* becomes a required area of excellence in order to quickly detect shifting needs in that user. Another critical skill is developing long-term *user loyalty* to the company's products.

Why is this concept of area excellence an integral part of strategic thinking? The reason is simple. No company has the resources to develop skills equally in all strategic areas that accompany each driving force. Therefore, strategic decision making relies on management's ability to clearly identify those two or three skills that are critical to the success of its strategy and give those areas preferential resources. In good times, these areas receive additional resources; in bad times, they are the last areas to cut. 3M, which can be considered a technology-driven company, has a chairman—Alan Jacobsen—who clearly recognizes this concept. When Jacobsen took over as chief executive officer, he set about to improve 3M's profitability. He asked all his division heads to cut expenses by as much as 35 percent, but he spared R & D expenditures. In fact, he increased R & D from 4.5 percent of sales to 6.6 percent. The reason: Research is a required area of excellence for a technology-driven company.

Another example is Wal-Mart, whose CEO, David D. Glass, says that the use of technology in its distribution centers has resulted in the fact that, "our distribution facilities are one of the keys to our success. If we do anything better than other folks, that's it." This is how it should be for a distribution-method driven company.

A third example is Merck, which is pursuing a technology-driven strategy—prescription drugs. In order for this strategy to succeed, such a company must excel at research, and CEO Ray Valgelos's company excels in four critical areas—biochemistry, neurology, immunology, and molecular biology—four describable skills that are given preferential resources at Merck.

ANTICIPATE THE IMPLICATIONS OF YOUR STRATEGY

Often, when a chief executive changes the strategy and direction of his or her organization, he or she does not take the time to think through the implications of that change. As a result, CEOs end up reacting to these changes as they encounter them. Every change in strategy—even a minor one—will bring about implications of one kind or another. If you want your strategy to succeed you must now devote some time and thought to identifying the issues that stand in the way of making your strategy work. What are all the changes that need to be addressed in order for the strategy to work? These changes become what we, at DPI, call strategic critical issues. These issues become management's agenda, and each issue is assigned to a specific person who becomes the "owner" of the issue and is held responsible and accountable for getting it resolved. My friends at 3M call issue resolution "pin the rose" time. It is the successful management and resolution of these issues over time that will assure the implementation of the strategy.

SUMMARY

Strategic thinking is the most important skill required of a chief executive officer and leader of an organization. Followers generally do not follow leaders blindly, and unless a leader can articulate his or her vision and get the commitment of followers to it, he or she forge ahead alone.

In a recent book called *The Leader-Manager,* William D. Hilt reported on a survey conducted to identify some common characteristics of leaders across cultures and organizations. From his study, he concluded that four basic traits appeared in all leaders, irrespective of organization or country.

1. The leader had a clear vision for the organization.
2. The leader had the ability to communicate this vision to others.
3. The leader had the ability to motivate others to work toward the vision.
4. The leader had the ability to "work the system" to get things done.

Although we agree with these four characteristics, our experience shows that leaders have great difficulty articulating their strategy and vision to others. Thus, it becomes imperative for the leader to clearly understand the *process* of strategic thinking in order to involve others in the development of the strategy. This is how motivation, commitment, and successful implementation will result.

4

The Leader as Innovator

Innovation is the fuel of corporate longevity. Without continuous innovation, organizations sputter and die. Nonetheless, most organizations practice innovation in a haphazard manner, apparently hoping that it will happen. In a 1990 DPI survey of two hundred Fortune 500 companies, two-thirds said they had no formal program to encourage the search for and development of new products, customers, or markets.

The United States, as mentioned in chapter 1, is losing its innovative prowess. However, there are some U.S. corporations that are still among the world's best. Caterpillar, 3M, Hewlett Packard, and Johnson & Johnson seem to have an infinite ability to churn out new products at a dizzying pace, which means that the skill is not dead. In fact, in the most successful companies, innovation is a paranoiac need. The lifeline of any unregulated organization is its ability to continuously find opportunities for new products or services and to develop better processes to manufacture and deliver them.

One of the most important realizations of a leader is to recognize that the organization needs *two* management systems. One is used to run your existing businesses, and the second is used to develop concepts for new products, customers, and markets. Most organizations usually have systems and processes to run the existing businesses, but very few have a formal process to develop *new* ideas and concepts. At this point, some might say that innovation is a haphazard process that cannot be codified. However, our work has shown that if a person or an organization is good at a particular skill, there is a process being practiced, although it is usually by osmosis. As long as a skill is being practiced by osmosis it cannot be made into a repeatable business practice. It is for this reason that innovation happens, or seems to happen, in a haphazard manner in most organizations.

The leader's challenge, then, is to understand the process of innovative thinking in order to institutionalize it as a formal activity in the organization and to develop the skill in his or her subordinates.

CHANGE: THE RAW MATERIAL OF INNOVATION

Before describing the process of innovation, the leader must understand the role of *change* in this process. Change is the raw material of innovation. One cannot have innovation without it. There is a direct linear extrapolation between the amount of change found in an organization's business environment and the amount of innovation that is possible there. The more change, the more room for innovation, and the less change, the less innovation. Innovation thrives on change.

As a consequence, innovative leaders also thrive on change. Innovative leaders do not see change as bad but rather as a constant source of opportunity. The attitude that change is healthy is a key difference between a leader and most followers. Seeing change as healthy and as a constant source of opportunity is a critical mind-set that the leader must instill in his or her followers. Change, as the root of innovation, is a fundamental concept of innovation; consequently, assessing changes that affect the organization must be a deliberate process that is both promoted and practiced by its leader.

THE DIFFERENT FORMS OF INNOVATION

Innovation is a much misunderstood word. To some it means technological breakthroughs, while to others it means something akin to the "big bang" theory of the universe.

For the purpose of outlining a process of innovative thinking, we will attempt to describe the different forms that innovation can take. The first distinction that needs to be made is that between innovation and invention. Innovation is the broader concept of continuous improvement, whereas invention is one form of innovation. Inventions are usually associated with discoveries—technology, patents, formulas, and so forth. Inventions can lead to major breakthroughs. There are, however, many other forms of innovation that are more mundane but that, over time, can give an organization a sustainable competitive advantage. We will discuss these other forms in the following paragraphs. There are two areas of an organization in which innovation or invention can occur. The first is in the development of new products and/or the improvement of current ones, and is usually referred to as *product innovation*. The second is in the improvement of the processes that sell, manufacture, deliver, or service the products, and is usually referred to as *process innovation*.

In each of these two areas, we will build a case to demonstrate that the best leaders do not believe in "big bang" innovation but rather in the more mundane approach of marginal, incremental, but continuous innovation to the organization's products and processes.

If you believe in the "big bang" approach to innovation, namely invention—it will be a long time between "bangs." One industry that practices this approach is the pharmaceutical industry, in which a new prescription product comes along every dozen years or so. On the other hand, 3M had hundreds of different versions of its Post-it note pads within months of producing its original yellow, finger-size format. Each additional version was only a marginal, incremental improvement over the previous one. Nonetheless, it is this ability to continuously innovate that gives 3M an edge over its competitors.

One of the primary tasks of an effective leader (if the organization is to perpetuate itself) is to install a deliberate process of systematic innovation and provide management mechanisms that assure its practice on a continuous basis by everyone in the organization.

THE INNOVATIVE THINKING PROCESS

The innovation process has four distinct steps:

- *Search*. Innovative leaders and organizations know where to look in their environments for changes that can be converted into opportunities for new products, customers, or markets, or for ways to improves its processes.
- *Assessment*. Innovative leaders and organizations know how to assess opportunities against four key criteria in order to rank opportunities in terms of their overall potential.
- *Development*. Innovative leaders and organizations can anticipate the critical factors that will lead to the success or failure of each opportunity.
- *Pursuit*. Innovative leaders and organizations can develop an implementation plan that promotes success and avoids failure.

THE FIRST STEP: SEARCH

"Where do you find all these new ideas?" we asked several of the most innovative people at 3M, Caterpillar, Johnson & Johnson, and other firms.

"Lightning bolts out of the blue," said one.

"Gut feeling," said another.

"Magic," responded a third person.

In other words, they did not know and could not attribute a source to their innovation. Interestingly, good innovators frequently cannot describe the process they use and therefore attribute the skill to all types of irrelevant occurrences. When we observed these people at work, however, we saw them practicing a very deliberate process that they used over and over but could not describe.

Good innovators know where to look for changes that lend themselves to ideas or concepts for new products or ways to improve the running of the business. There are ten specific areas of the business that they constantly monitor for changes that can be converted into new opportunities. (Peter Drucker first mentioned these changes in his book *Innovation and Entrepreneurship,* 1985.)

Unexpected Successes

Every organization has events that happen to it that succeed beyond anyone's wildest dreams. A product sells more briskly than anticipated in Montana. Market share goes through the roof in France. Wholesalers, to whom the firm had never expected to sell, start placing large orders. Unfortunately, in too many organizations unexpected successes are looked on as temporary aberrations that will quickly return to normal. In a recent interview in *Fortune* magazine, a senior manager at Caterpillar made this statement in regard to the unexpected high sales of their D9 tractor: "The surge of demand will begin to ease next year. It is an aberration" (December 19, 1988).

People who see unexpected successes as temporary aberrations will miss out on a number of future opportunities. The *right* question to ask is, "What caused this success and how can we spread it out over everything we do?"

Unexpected Failure

Again, every organization has events that cause it to fail miserably. In this case most people tend to spend the rest of their careers defending the failure. Instead, they should be asking, "What caused this failure and how can we turn it into an opportunity the next time?" A striking example to follow is Ford, which was responsible for the worst new product introduction ever—the Edsel. However, the automaker was smart enough to learn from this failure and, only a few years later, introduced the most successful new car to date—the Mustang.

Unexpected External Events

IBM was merrily following its five-year business plan when Apple introduced the personal computer (PC). To IBM, this was a totally unexpected event. IBM was, therefore, faced with two options: one was to ignore the event, while the second, which it wisely chose, was to "tweak" its business plan a little and introduce a PC of its own, which became the industry leader. The right question in this instance is "How can we turn this external event into a new product or customer?"

Process Weaknesses

All organizations are composed of various processes, procedures, or systems: A sales order entry system, an accounts payable system, a manufacturing process, a distribution system, a quality audit process, a sales refund procedure, an inventory control system, and so forth. Every process or system in existence has one of three things wrong with it:

1. a bottleneck,
2. a weak link, or
3. a missing link.

If we spend a little time identifying and describing the various processes that exist in our organization and then ask, "What bottlenecks, weak links, or missing links are there in these processes and how can we eliminate them?" the query will surely give rise to a number of innovative solutions that will make these processes more effective.

Industry/Structure Changes

When the "rules of the game" are suddenly changed in an industry, the changes will usually bring on turmoil, meaning threats for some but opportunities for others. When deregulation hit the health care and transportation industries, many firms and executives in these businesses saw only the threats associated with these changes. Some, like Humana Corporation or Dave Burr of People's Express saw opportunity. The right question, then, is, "How can we transform these structural changes that are happening in our industry into new products, customers, or markets?"

High-Growth Areas

Companies need growth in order to perpetuate themselves. Therefore, they need opportunities that could bring more growth than what might be considered normal. To this end, we should search for changes in the present business or related businesses in which growth is occurring faster than two factors—growth in gross national product (GNP) growth or population growth. These are the areas that will bring opportunities with exceptional growth. Why are there as many as 140 PC manufacturers?

The reason is simple. The demand for PCs is growing at a rate of 25 to 50 percent per year. In this kind of environment, there is bound to be a lot of turmoil, which will create opportunity.

Converging Technologies

When two or more technologies start to merge, that convergence is bound to produce turmoil and, as a result, opportunity. The convergence of telecommunication and computer technologies that we have been witnessing for the last fifteen years created turmoil which was perceived initially by AT&T as a major threat but was perceived as a major opportunity by NEC, Northern Telecom, Mitel, and Rolm. Rather than attempt to defend itself against these opportunities, as AT&T did (to its regret), these organizations sought to encourage this change with products and services that exploited it.

Demographic Changes

The demographics of an organization's customers are not static: They change with time. As a result, if we attempt to anticipate the demographic changes that will occur in its customer base in the future, we are bound to find opportunity. For example, if we look at the current phenomenon of the aging of America, we should be able to see nothing but opportunities. As the population grows older, there will be new opportunities resulting from the following needs:

1. Financial counseling advice to manage and reinvest monies coming from individual retirement accounts (IRAs) and other programs,
2. Specially tailored travel packages,
3. Special "fountain of youth" medicines,
4. Counseling services to help younger couples take care of aging parents, and
5. Special living facilities for elderly people over age one hundred (there are already thirty-five thousand in the United States today).

There are four categories of demographic changes that need to be monitored in a firm's customers.

1. Income,
2. Age,
3. Education, and
4. Mix.

The right question is, "What demographic changes are happening or will happen in our customers in these four areas, and how can we convert these into new opportunities?"

Perception Changes

The way in which your customers perceive your products changes with time. If you can anticipate the changes of perception that your customers have or will have vis-à-vis your products, you are bound to find opportunity. For example, the automobile was once perceived strictly as a mode of transport. In the 1960s, however, Ford's Lee Iacocca detected that some people perceived the automobile to be a reflection of their lifestyles, and came out with the Mustang—the first "life-style" car. Now there is the BMW for the "Yuppies," the Volvo for the safety-conscious, and so on. Ten years ago, microfilm was perceived as "high tech," and 3M had a thriving business. Today, microfilm is perceived as "low tech," and 3M is struggling because electronics is now preferred as high tech, even though microfilm is a better product for archiving large quantities of data.

The right question to ask is, "What changes are happening in how our customers perceive our products, and how can we convert these changes into new opportunities?"

New Knowledge

New knowledge means inventions, discoveries, patents, and the like. Obviously discoveries, or new knowledge, will always lead to opportunities in the form of new products or markets. However, inventions can take a long time to commercialize into profitable products. Fiber optics and lasers were invented in 1955 and are only now beginning to be converted into successful products. History has shown that inventions can take as long as twenty-five years to become commercially viable. Therefore, it is wise to seek innovations in some of the other nine areas first.

Observations Regarding the Search Step

During our work with client organizations, we have made several critical observations regarding how these companies go about finding opportunities. First, all the organizations with which we have worked to date were bombarded by changes from all ten areas simultaneously. Lesson number one in corporate life is that no organization is immune to change. The only constant is change, and any organization that tries to hide or protect itself from change through regulation, legislation, or artificial barriers is doomed to complacency and eventual failure. As much as some people may resent it, innovation is creative destruction of the status quo, something that the best leaders are constantly looking to disrupt.

Second, the best leaders do not wait for these changes to occur before responding. In fact, wherever applicable, they will be the ones to initiate them.

Third, there is a direct relationship between the probability of finding opportunity and its source on the list of ten search areas. The further down the list you must go to find opportunity, the less likely you will be to succeed. The reason is simple: The further it is down the list, the more difficult the change will be to detect and to convert into a successful opportunity. Nonetheless, this is where we found many organizations looking, at the expense of passing by a host of potential opportunities from the top of the list which are easier to detect and exploit.

Fourth, most organizations that were being bombarded by these ten types of changes had the tendency to see only the threats associated with them, overlooking the opportunities. It was usually people outside the organization who saw the opportunities. An effective leader deals with the threats but demands that the organization and its people translate these changes into opportunities as well. As Peter Drucker wrote, "Resources, to produce results, must be allocated to opportunities rather than to problems" (*Innovation and Entrepreneurship,* 1985).

Last, strong leaders do not count on home runs or the "big bang" approach to innovation. If they do come across "big bang" ideas, all the better. In the meantime, however, they believe in and practice continuous, marginal, incremental innovation in every aspect of the business and on the part of everyone in the organization.

In an article entitled "Tough Minded Ways to Get Innovative," Andrall E. Pearson talked about innovation at Hasbro, one of the most successful and innovative toy companies. He said:

Unlike most of its competitors, Hasbro doesn't focus on inventing new blockbuster toys. Its management will take blockbusters if they come along, of course. But the company doesn't spend the bulk of its product development dollars on such long-odds bets. Instead, it centers its efforts on staple-toy lines like G.I. Joe, Transformers, games and preschool basics that can be extended and renewed each year. (*Harvard Business Review,* May/June 1988)

THE SECOND STEP: ASSESSMENT

As a result of the search step, we now face a multitude of opportunities. As any good innovator knows, not all opportunities are worth pursuing. The second step of innovation is to assess all the opportunities against certain criteria in order to rank them in terms of their potential to the organization.

The first two criteria are obvious enough—cost and benefit. Each opportunity needs to be assessed in terms of its relative cost versus benefit ratio. In fact, a visual grid (the Assessment Grid) can be used to show where each opportunity falls.

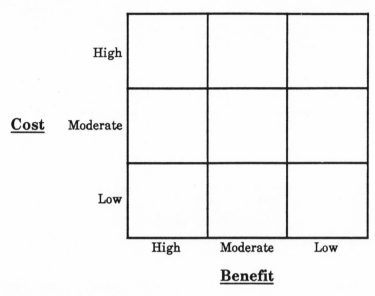

- What is the cost of this opportunity?
- What is the benefit of this opportunity?

The next two assessment criteria are less obvious—those of strategic fit and difficulty of implementation. These two criteria are probably more important than the cost/benefit ratio, but unfortunately, they are almost always overlooked.

How well does this opportunity fit the strategy of the business? This is a key question that is often not asked, but should be. Experience has shown that organizations that try to innovate outside the strategic framework of the business usually do not succeed. An example is Exxon's attempt to diversify into office equipment. The reason is simple. In order to succeed in its core strategic business, an organization develops skills, structures, and systems that are not usually transferable to opportunities outside this framework. A senior executive of Exxon recently told us that Exxon executives did not understand the office equipment business as well as they did the "trivia of the oil business," and thus could not manage or even judge the opportunities of the former. There was no strategic fit.

THE ESSENCE OF LEADERSHIP

One can now add the strategic fit criterion to the Assessment Grid.

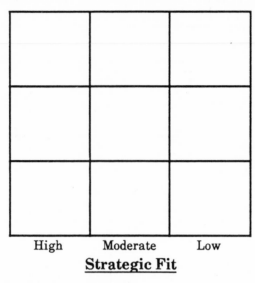

Strategic Fit

The fourth criterion is difficulty of implementation. Again, we have seen many good opportunities fail because management had simply understated the degree of difficulty in trying to capitalize on an opportunity. The grid can now be used to assess difficulty of implementation.

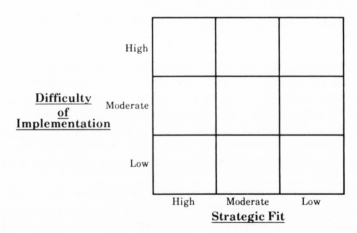

When we superimpose the cost/benefit grid over the strategic/difficulty of implementation grid, we now have an objective ranking of the potential of each opportunity under review.

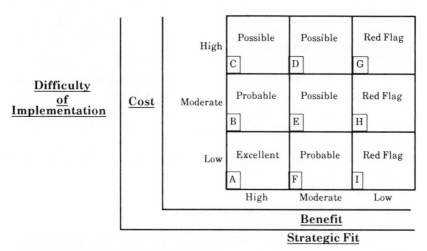

Certain conclusions can now be drawn. Obviously, an opportunity that falls in quadrant A on all four criteria is the best we will find—low in cost, high in benefit, good in strategic fit, and easy to implement. There is none better. Opportunities in quadrant B and F are probable. B quadrant opportunities are characterized by higher costs and more difficult implementation. Quadrant F opportunities are likely to stray from the strategy of the business and bring less benefit. Quadrant C opportunities bring very high costs together with a high difficulty of implementation. The opportunities in quadrants G, H, and I obviously are risky because they violate most of the four criteria.

Presented with such an assessment, the leader of an organization should use it to read the thought process of his subordinates. For example, if an opportunity falls in quadrant D (but something about that opportunity attracts you to it), the grid specifies exactly what must be done to the opportunity before it can be pursued.

First, a way must be found to make it fit the strategy of the business (a move to the left). Second, ways must be found to reduce the costs (one or two moves down). Third, ways must be found to decrease the difficulty of implementation (one or two moves down). If we can affect these three variables, we can move the opportunity to quadrant A and it will become viable. If not, it should be left where it is.

As a result of applying the assessment grid to all the opportunities, the best ones—like cream—will migrate to the top of the list. There are the ones that we now want to take through the final two steps of the innovation process.

THE THIRD STEP: DEVELOPMENT

Few organizations have in place a formal process to generate and assess new opportunities. Fewer still have the ability to capitalize on these opportunities successfully. This is the reason for the next two steps in the innovation process, which concentrate on anticipating the critical elements that will ensure the successful pursuit of good opportunities.

The development step has two phases. Each opportunity, starting with the best one first, is now examined, and best and worst case scenarios are constructed using the results we could expect were we to pursue this opportunity. The questions asked are:

- "If we pursued this opportunity, what are all the best results this opportunity would bring?" (best case scenario)
- "If we pursued this opportunity, what are all the worst results this opportunity would bring?" (worst case scenario)

The results are listed as follows:

Worst Case Scenario   **Best Case Scenario**

_____   _____
_____   _____
_____   _____
_____   _____
_____   _____

At this point, another filter is brought into the process: It is called the risk/reward analysis. The risk/reward analysis is a simple scale that looks like this.

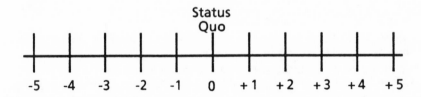

One can now ask some additional questions of each opportunity:

- "Compared to where we are now (the status quo), where will the best case scenario take us?"
- "Compared to where we are now (the status quo), where will the worst case scenario take us?"

There are a variety of permutations and combinations that can serve as answers to these two questions, however, here are a few possibilities:

- Best Case: +5
  Worst Case: +1

  Conclusion: No risk. Even if we achieve only the worst case results, we will be better off than we are today.

- Best Case: +1
  Worst Case: −5

  Conclusion: High risk. There is much more to lose than there is to gain. Is it worth the effort?

- Best Case: −1
  Worst Case: −5

  Conclusion: How can an opportunity, which is a good thing, take us back from the status quo? Sometimes it happens. A case in point is an opportunity our own firm explored a couple of years ago. One of our competitors, which was three times our size, became available for purchase. Obviously, this was an attractive opportunity since we could have quadrupled our business overnight. However, that particular competitor came with a bad reputation in the marketplace, and we felt that we would not only acquire the competitor but its reputation as well. This we felt, would set us back from where we were (the status quo). We declined.

- Best Case: +3
  Worst Case: −2

  Conclusion: If one factor falls on the plus side and the other on the minus side, we must look at the spread between the two. A (+1, −4) is obviously not as good as a (+4, −1).

The result of using risk/reward analysis is that we now can home in on the "crème de la crème" of opportunities. At the top of our list now are the very best of all the opportunities available.

THE FOURTH STEP: PURSUIT

The final step of the innovation process is to construct an implementation plan that will avoid the worst case scenario and ensure that the best case scenario will occur. Again, this step has three phases.

Phase one is to take both scenarios (best and worst) from the development step and ask:

- "What critical factors could cause the worst case scenario?"
- "What critical factors could cause the best case scenario?"

The critical factors that could cause either scenario are listed as follows:

Worst Case Scenario   **Likely Causes (Critical Factors)**
_____   _____
_____   _____
_____   _____
_____   _____

Best Case Scenario   **Likely Causes (Critical Factors)**
_____   _____
_____   _____
_____   _____
_____   _____

The second phase is then to anticipate actions that could prevent the worst case scenario from occurring and promote the occurrence of the best case scenario. Both preventive and promotive actions must be aimed at the likely causes since these are critical factors that will bring about either best case or worst case results.

Worst Case Scenario   **Likely Causes**   **Preventive Actions**
_____   _____ _____
_____   _____ _____
_____   _____ _____
_____   _____ _____

Best Case Scenario   **Likely Causes**   **Promotive Actions**
_____   _____ _____
_____   _____ _____
_____   _____ _____
_____   _____ _____

The third and final phase of the process is to construct a plan to pursue each opportunity that is still on the list. The plan is a breakdown of the implementation steps or activities needed to implement each opportunity. In the plan, we should include both the promotable and preventive actions identified above. The inclusion of these will ensure that the worst case

results will be avoided and the best case results achieved. The plan might
have this format:

Opportunity: _____
Owner: _____

Plan Steps	Completion Date	Responsible	Contributors
1.			
2.			
3.			
4.			
5.			
6.			
7.			
8.			
9.			
10.			

The process described in this chapter can make innovation happen on a
continuous basis. The leader's role is to provide a forum and a framework
within which it can occur. This means conducting meetings (forums) in
which part of the agenda is dedicated to searching for opportunities together with a formal process (framework) that makes it happen.

John Gardner, in his 1963 book *Self-Renewal,* said that to have renewal
you need the seemingly exclusive conditions of stability and innovation,
because stability without innovation is stagnation, while innovation without stability is anarchy. He argued that you need to have innovation in
content and stability in process, and we concur.

Niccolò Machiavelli once described the innovative person in this way:
"The innovator makes enemies of all those who prospered under the old
order, and only lukewarm support is forthcoming from those who would
prosper under the new." Since we view innovation as "creative destruction" of the status quo, it is easy to understand why people who benefit
from the status quo are threatened by it. However, there is no other
alternative to progress. Change can be made less threatening to people if
it is accompanied by a conscious and visible process.

5

The Leader as Decision Maker

Once a strategy is in place and innovative opportunities have been targeted, a leader is left with the mundane task of running the business on a day-to-day basis. All kinds of operational issues will surface while he or she is trying to keep the locomotive on track, which demand yet another set of mental skills as part of the leader's arsenal. What is now required is rational decision making. The best way to explain the different components of this process is to describe how it evolved.

AMBUSHED BY OPERATIONAL ISSUES

From the time when a person enters his or her office each morning, he or she is constantly bombarded with a variety of issues that need to be addressed. These issues come in various forms:

—Memos,
—Mail,
—Telephone messages,
—Reports,
—Faxes,
—Telexes,
—Meeting notices, and
—Overnight mail.

This is true of a president, a general manager, a middle manager, a secretary, a supervisor, an operator, or even a janitor. Therefore, the first thing any of these people do each morning is to take inventory of these various issues in order to come up with a list of things to do. In other words, they place the issues in order of priority. Some of us do it mentally, while others do it visually—on paper. Then we start working down the list. If, by 10:00 A.M., we have resolved the first four items on the list, guess what happens next? You're right: Six more issues suddenly appear. A first observation we made in our observations was that people in business are under a continuous bombardment of different issues, which continues relentlessly, day after day, and year after year.

However, if a person were to "stop the world" at 10:01 A.M. and take stock or "take a picture" of the different issues on his or her desk, he or she would find only three types of issues which present themselves over and over, each of which is associated with the element of time.

The first type of issue is one that comes from the past. When it lands on someone's desk, the event has already occurred. Why should an event that has already occurred end up on someone's list of things to do? Why should someone be concerned about an event that has already occurred? It is probably because the event represents something that has gone wrong, and this person is being asked to correct it. However, before being able to correct this situation, the individual needs to investigate what caused it to occur in the first place. This situation is called a problem, and the thought process required to solve it is called *Problem Analysis*. Problem Analysis is a diagnostic process used to find the cause of an event that has gone wrong for unknown reasons. Therefore, as a person sorts through the issues on his or her desk, a pile of "problem" issues starts emerging.

A second stack consists of issues whereby a person is being told to "do something." However, there may be different things to do or different courses of action available. In other words, there are several alternatives or options available, and the best option is not evident because all the alternatives look reasonably good. In this instance, a person is in the present tense and in a situation of choice. The thought process that will be used to bring the issue to a resolution is called *Decision Analysis*. Decision Analysis is a process used to choose the best option or course of action when several good ones are available.

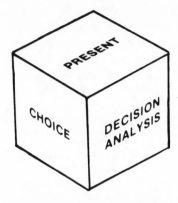

The third pile that will form on a person's desk consists of issues in which a tentative decision has been made by someone in the organization, and this person's responsibility is to implement it successfully. With this goal in mind, you develop a plan and then look ahead, into the future, to try to anticipate any elements that may stand in the way of the plan's success. If these potential problems can be anticipated, one can anticipate actions to prevent them from occurring. This third thought process is called *Potential Problem Analysis,* and is used to plan and implement decisions successfully.

Thus, an inventory of all the issues that face a person in business can be catalogued into three types, with each type requiring a different mode of thinking. The conscious application of the appropriate process to each issue is at the heart of rational decision making and is the key to getting operational issues resolved quickly and successfully. Therefore, it is very important that we have a mental compass to situate ourselves in the right process before we start any analysis.

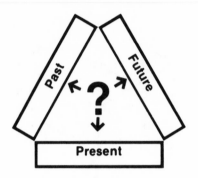

SITUATION ANALYSIS

Situation Analysis is a process to help us do exactly what it says—situate ourselves in our thought process. Let us look at its logic path:

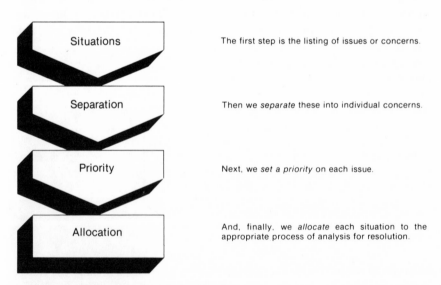

The first step is the listing of issues or concerns.

Then we *separate* these into individual concerns.

Next, we *set a priority* on each issue.

And, finally, we *allocate* each situation to the appropriate process of analysis for resolution.

Situations

Every person carries a list of issues or concerns that need to be dealt with. Some of us have a formal list—we keep it on our desk pad or diary, or on a list of things to do today. Many of us do it informally, in our heads. The first step of Situation Analysis involves this list of daily concerns. We define a concern as any situation—whether threat or opportunity—that can have an impact on the results we are trying to achieve.

Separation

Many of the issues that we need to address tend to be general; they are messy and fuzzy in nature. We have to apply Caesar's principle of "divide and conquer" in order to resolve each one. This is known as separation. It is the technique of breaking large, complex situations into smaller, more manageable ones. We separate fuzzy issues until we have discrete issues that are distinct from each other and can be handled on an individual basis.

Set Priorities

The previous step of separation means that we now have more issues to deal with. Since even Albert Einstein admitted that he could only do one thing at a time, we must now set priorities on these issues. There are various ways of setting priorities. Let us look at some of the wrong ones. There is the technique of first-in, first-out, which means that whatever came into the basket first gets immediate attention. There is the opposite concept of last-in, first-out, in which the last item in gets immediate attention. A third is the technique of the "squeaky wheel." Whoever yells the loudest gets his concern addressed first. Likewise, the medium used may give undue priority to an issue. A message received by telegram rather than by mail may receive priority. However, if we want to set priorities correctly, there are three elements to examine.

First, we should look at the seriousness.

• How important or serious is the issue?

Next, we should look at the urgency.

• What is the time deadline for resolving it?
• What urgency does it have?

Last, we should explore the growth.

• If we do nothing, what will happen to the seriousness?

Applying these three components to each issue will help us set priorities correctly.

Allocate

Once we have our concerns arranged in order of priority, the last step is to allocate each issue to the appropriate process of analysis. Three questions are used to do this:

1. Do we want to know the cause of this situation? If the answer is "yes," then the process required for resolution is Problem Analysis.
2. Is there a need to select the best option? If we answer "yes," then Decision Analysis is required.
3. Do we want to assure the success of our plan? A "yes" would lead us to Potential Problem Analysis.

Situation Analysis is the hub of our thinking. It is the mental compass of our logic map. It directs us to the proper analytical process in order to get issues and situations resolved successfully.

PROBLEM ANALYSIS

Let us, for a moment, situate ourselves in the past. When we talk about analyzing a problem situation, we want to go from problem to action.

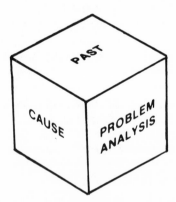

As in traveling, there are a number of steps that we may have to pursue along that path. That is called the logic path of Problem Analysis (PA).

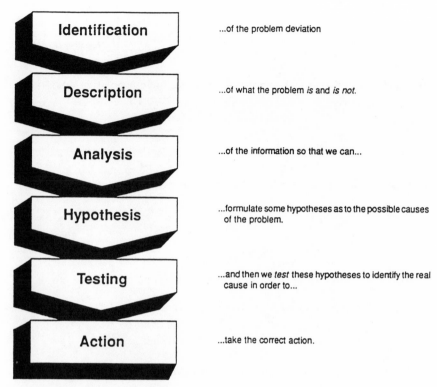

Identification   ...of the problem deviation

Description   ...of what the problem *is* and *is not.*

Analysis   ...of the information so that we can...

Hypothesis   ...formulate some hypotheses as to the possible causes of the problem.

Testing   ...and then we *test* these hypotheses to identify the real cause in order to...

Action   ...take the correct action.

Let us now take a look at the skills involved in each of the steps of the Problem Analysis Logic Path.

Identification

The first step is, of course, identification. "How do I know I have a problem?" One way of looking at a problem is to say that some obstacle is interfering with the attainment of some goal, or that some deviation has occurred in the expected performance, or norm. The first element involved is to identify the norm. Another element that is involved is the knowledge of what is actually being achieved or what is actually happening.

Norm = Actual: No Problem

When the norm and the actual are one and the same, there is no problem. When the actual is lower than the norm, however, we have a negative deviation.

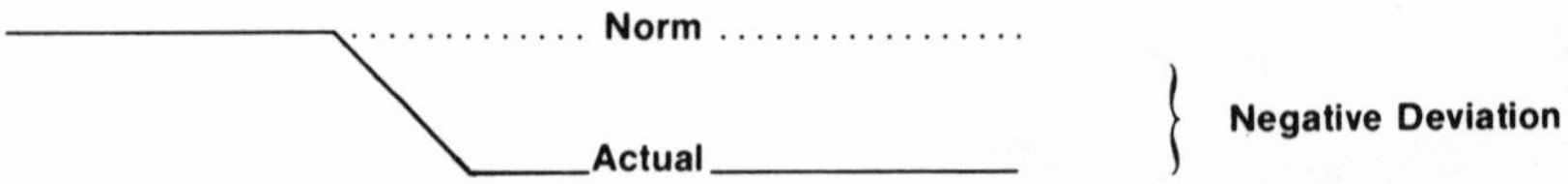

When the actual is above the norm, then we have a positive deviation.

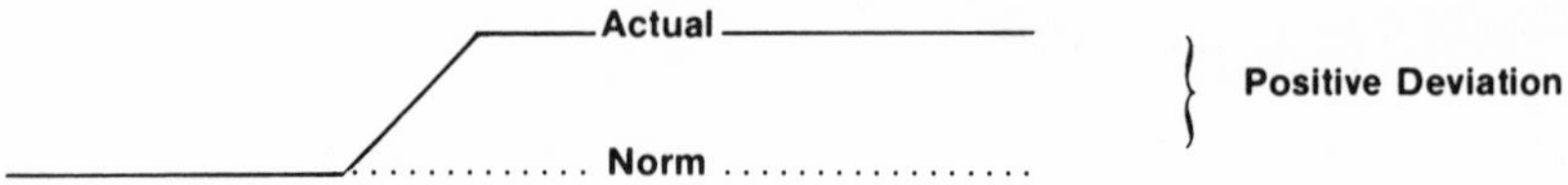

The first thing we will notice about the deviation is its effects.

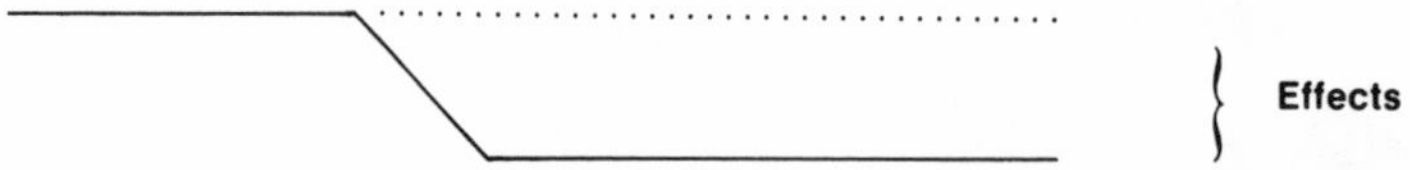

However, in order to correct a deviation, we need to find the cause.

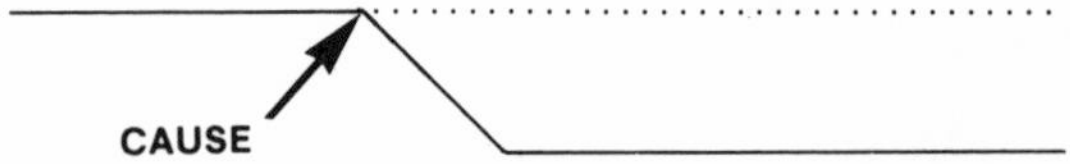

To do that, we must proceed to a description of the problem.

Description

To properly describe a problem, there are four dimensions about which we can get some information. These are the identity, location, timing, and extent of the problem. The following are questions designed to help us describe the problem.

The first set of questions is designed to help identify the object/unit involved in the problem and the defect seen:

PROBLEM DESCRIPTION

	PROBLEM AREA	NON-PROBLEM AREA
	IS	IS NOT
IDENTITY	WHAT Object • What is the problem unit/object/thing?	• What could the problem unit be but is not?
	Defect • What is wrong with it? • What is the defect/fault?	• What else could be wrong with it but is not? • What other defect/fault could there be but is not?

The following questions are designed to help us geographically locate the problem:

		IS	IS NOT
L O C A T I O N		**WHERE** **Object** • Where can the problem be found/ noticed/observed/reported?	• Where else could the problem be but is not?
		Defect • Where is the defect/fault on the unit?	• Where else could the defect/fault be but is not?

The following questions are designed to help us determine the timing of the problem:

		IS	IS NOT
T I M I N G		**WHEN** **Object** • When was the problem first observed?	• When else could the problem have been observed but was not?
		Defect • When in the life/operation cycle is the defect/fault observed? • What is the pattern?	• When else could the defect/fault be seen but was not? • What could the pattern be but is not?

The following questions are designed to help us determine the magnitude of the problem:

		IS	IS NOT
E X T E N T		**HOW MUCH, MANY** **Object** • How many objects/units are defective?	• How many objects/units could be defective but are not?
		Defect • How many defects/faults on the object/ unit? • How much of the object/unit is defective? • What is the trend?	• How many defects/faults could there be but are not? • How much of the object/unit could be defective but is not? • What could the trend be but is not?

By describing the problem in terms of what it is (problem area) and what it is not (non-problem area), we are able to put sharper boundaries around the problem. These boundaries will help us through the next step.

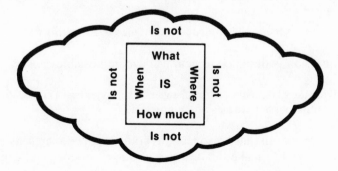

Analysis

The first part of the analysis step is to compare the problem area to the nonproblem area, or, in other words, the *is* to the *is not*. We can compare for similarities or we can compare for differences. In looking for new and additional information, experience has shown that comparing for differences is more helpful. In particular, we should examine our description to look for differences in areas in which there are sharp contrasts in the information.

The following questions are designed to help us to identify differences:

- What is different, distinctive, or unique between *what* the problem is and what it is not?
- What is different, distinctive, or unique between *where* the problem is and where it is not?
- What is different, distinctive, or unique between *when* the problem is seen and when it is not?

The next step is to examine the differences in order to identify changes that have occurred. The search for the cause must center itself on these changes. If no change had occurred, we would not have a problem. To narrow our search for relevant changes, we should limit our search to looking for changes within the differences that we have identified between the problem area and the nonproblem area.

The following question is designed to help us do this:

- What has changed about each of these differences?

Noting the date of each change is also helpful, as we might be able to relate the start of a problem to a specific change that occurred.

Hypotheses

From our analysis of the deviation we can now formulate some hypotheses as to the possible causes of the deviation. Hypotheses are a combination of:

Changes Identified + Experience + Expertise

This question is designed to help us develop possible causes.

- In studying the differences and/or changes, what hypotheses can be drawn that might identify possible causes of the problem?

At this stage, we list all reasonable hypotheses. The emphasis is to be constructive and to make the best use of our experience and expertise.

Test

It is now time to test our possible causes in order to eliminate those that are not related to the problem. We screen each possible cause through our description. If a possible cause cannot explain both sides of the description, it is not likely to be the real cause. Some possible causes might do so if we add certain assumptions ("only if"). In such cases these assumptions should be noted.

The testing technique is as follows:

• Test each possible cause through the test bed (description), especially the sharp contrast areas.
• Note all assumptions ("only if") that you have to construct to support your hypotheses.

The most probable cause will be the one that best explains the description, or the one with the least number of assumptions. To be 100 percent certain, we must now verify our assumptions—which can be done quickly and inexpensively. The question is simple:

• How can you quickly and cheaply verify your assumptions?

Should these assumptions prove to be true, we have the root cause of the problem and are ready to take action.

Action

To address a problem, we can take three different types of action.

Interim Action	This is used to buy us time while we search out the cause of the problem. Interim action is aimed at the effects of the problem.
Adaptive Action	We decide to live with the problem or adapt ourselves to the problem. Adaptive action is also aimed at the effects of the problem.
Corrective Action	This is the only action designed to eliminate the problem. It is aimed at the cause of the problem.

PROBLEM ANALYSIS

LOGIC PATH	PROCESS QUESTIONS
DEVIATION IDENTIFICATION	• What is the deviation?
DESCRIPTION	• What is/is not the problem? • Where is/is not the problem? • When is/is not the problem seen? • How much of a problem do we have/have not?
ANALYSIS	• What differences/changes fall out of the description?
HYPOTHESES	• What are the possible causes?
TESTING	• How well does each cause explain the description? • Which is the most probable cause? • How can we verify our assumptions?
ACTION	• What action do we take?

PROBLEM ANALYSIS WORKSHEET

DEVIATION: NORM/STANDARD _____ **ACTUAL** _____

PROBLEM STATEMENT (OBJECT/DEFECT) _____

		DESCRIPTION					
	IS	*	IS NOT	DIFFERENCES	CHANGES	DATE	POSSIBLE CAUSES

IDENTITY	WHAT						
	OBJECT						
	DEFECT						
LOCATION	WHERE						
	OBJECT						
	DEFECT						
TIMING	WHEN						
	OBJECT						
	DEFECT						
EXTENT	HOW MUCH						
	OBJECT						
	DEFECT						

TESTING
If this is the cause
how does it explain
that . . . ?

MOST PROBABLE CAUSE	VERIFICATION	ACTION

DECISION ANALYSIS

Let us now, for a moment, situate ourselves mentally in the present.

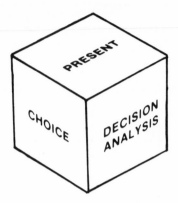

After we have explored the past to identify the cause of the problem, it is necessary to choose the appropriate course of action to address that problem. This next step in decision making is known as Decision Analysis. The overall objective in this process is to take several alternatives and choose the best one. The following is the *logic path of Decision Analysis*.

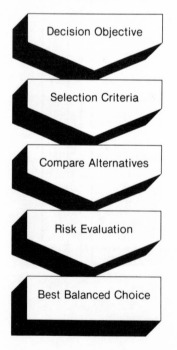

The first step in the process is to establish a *decision objective* or a decision statement.

In order to evaluate alternatives, we need to compare against *something*. We need to formulate certain *selection criteria* against which we will test our alternatives.

The next step is to compare alternatives. We now want to *screen the alternatives* through our selection criteria and eliminate the alternatives that don't give us satisfactory performance. From this step we have reduced the number of alternatives.

It is important now to evaluate the *risks* that are attached to each of these remaining alternatives.

The final step of decision analysis is making the *best balanced choice*. This involves reviewing the degree of risk in each alternative and judging whether or not we are prepared to take that risk. The best balanced choice is the alternative that performs the best against our selection criteria, together with the amount of risk that we are willing to accept.

Decision Objective

There are three elements of the decision objective or decision statement that we should keep in mind. The first element is the purpose. A decision statement should be formulated in terms that represents the purpose of what the analysis is about. It should represent an end result. As an example to demonstrate the process, let us assume that you have been mandated with the following decision by your company: Choose the best word processing system.

From time to time we may insert in our decision statement a word that restricts the range of alternatives that will be available to us. These words are called modifiers. Without modifiers, the range of alternatives would be broader. However, by adding a modifier we restrict the range. It is important to make sure when we formulate decision statements to examine them for modifiers to ensure that we do in fact want to include them. In the above example, we might wish to include the word "new," which obviously would eliminate second-hand systems.

The third element to consider about the decision objective or decision statement is the level of the decision. Most decisions stem from prior decisions. The higher the level of our decision, the greater the range of alternatives available to us. The lower the level, the more restricted is the range of alternatives. The level at which we start our decision dramatically changes the class of alternatives that we end up comparing. It enables us to compare similar classes of alternatives so that we compare apples to apples and not apples to oranges.

Selection Criteria

The second step in the logic path of Decision Analysis is to establish some criteria for selecting the best alternative. To generate effective selection criteria, we must ask four questions.

- What results do we want to achieve?
- What results do we want to avoid?
- What resources are available to spend?
- What resources do we want to preserve?

DECISION OBJECTIVE: _____

SELECTION CRITERIA WORKSHEET

RESULTS	RESOURCES
• What results do we want to *achieve*?	• What resources can we *spend*?
•What results do we want to *avoid*?	• What resources do we wish to *preserve*?

Once we have a list of selection criteria, we examine them to determine the criteria that are absolutely mandatory to the success of our decision. We classify our criteria into those that must absolutely be met and those that we want to achieve—that are desirable but not mandatory. The first criteria we list are the *musts*—those that are imperative and must be met by all available alternatives.

Then we take a look at the desirable criteria, or the *wants,* and weigh them in order of importance. By looking at our desirable criteria, we identify the one that is the most important to us and give it a weight of 10. With that as the benchmark, we weigh the others on a scale of 10 to 1, according to their relative importance.

DECISION OBJECTIVE: _____
CLASSIFICATION WORKSHEET

Which selection criteria are mandatory? Are they realistic?
How will we measure them?

MUSTS

_____
_____
_____
_____
_____

Which selection criteria are desirable but not mandatory?

WANTS	WEIGHT

NOTE: Have the *musts* been inverted into *wants?*

Compare Alternatives

The next step in the process of Decision Analysis is the step of comparing the alternatives. We must filter the alternatives through the selection criteria and eliminate those that do not measure up. Because we have classified our criteria into *musts* and *wants*, the first filter is to screen the alternatives against the *musts*.

Since we have set specific limits on these *musts*, we need to gather information about each alternative to see how well it complies with them. By comparing the information that is available about each alternative against each *must*, we can then make a go–no go decision. *Go* means that the alternative meets the limits that we have determined to be nonnegotiable and *no go* means that the alternative does not. The purpose of *must* criteria is to quickly screen out those alternatives that violate limits that we consider nonnegotiable, and thereby to reduce our range of alternatives.

The next step is to compare the remaining alternatives against the *wants*, or the desirable criteria. Again, the technique is to get information about the alternative that tells us how well it performs against each of our *wants*. We then use our judgment in assessing that information in order to score the performance of each alternative against each *want*. (See Decision Analysis Worksheet, below.) Using numbers to reflect our judgment, we give the top score to the alternative that performs the best followed by relative scores to each of the subsequent next best performing alternatives. We then proceed to do that against each *want*. By then multiplying the weight of the *wants* by the score of the alternative, we get a weighted score. We repeat the procedure for each *want*. Adding the total of these weighted scores gives us an index of performance. Thus, the step of comparing alternatives involves comparing our alternatives first against our *musts,* and then scoring their performance against our *wants* and eliminating those alternatives that give us poor performance. By now, we will have narrowed our choice down to one, two, or possibly three alternatives that perform substantially better than the rest.

Risk Evaluation

The next step in the Decision Analysis process is the step called risk evaluation. Every alternative or course of action considered brings with it certain risks. Therefore, in the analysis of the alternatives it is very important to evaluate the risks that are attached to each of these remaining alternatives. The technique is simple. We take each alternative and ask, "What risks do we face if we go with this alternative?" We list those risks. We do this for each of the remaining alternatives.

The risks will be different for each alternative because different alternatives bring different risks. However, there are different degrees of risk. First we look at the degree of probability that any of these risks will come about. Using a scale of high, medium, or low, or of 1 to 10, we examine each risk and assess its probability of occurrence. The next element in determining the degree of risk is to determine the degree of seriousness should it occur. If this risk occurs, what will be the impact of our particular decision? Using the same scale, we can then assess the degree of seriousness for each risk.

The Best Balanced Choice

The last step of Decision Analysis is making the best balanced choice. This means reviewing the risks that are represented by the probability and the seriousness. If our comfort level is such that we are not willing to undertake high risk, we would then have to choose an alternative that has attached to it a degree of risk with which we are comfortable. The best balanced choice becomes the alternative that performs the best, or reasonably well, against our selection criteria, together with the amount of risk that we are willing to accept.

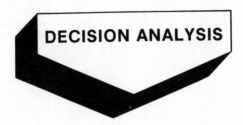

DECISION ANALYSIS

LOGIC PATH

DECISION OBJECTIVE

SELECTION CRITERIA

COMPARE ALTERNATIVES

RISK EVALUATION

BEST BALANCED CHOICE

PROCESS QUESTIONS

- What is the decision objective?

- What are the *musts*?
- What are the *wants* and their relative weight?

- What are all the alternatives?
- Are we satisfied with the quality of the options?
- Do we need to create new or better options?
- Do the alternatives meet the *musts*?
- How well do they perform against the *wants*?
- Which alternative(s) gives us the best overall performance?

- What are the risks?
- What is the degree of risk?
- What can be done to minimize these risks?

- What is the best balanced choice?

DECISION ANALYSIS WORKSHEET

OBJECTIVE: SELECT BEST WORD PROCESSOR

CRITERIA			ALTERNATIVES										
MUSTS < Minimum requirements Absolute constraints • Non-Negotiable • Limits • Measurable			How well does each alternative meet each *must?*										
			A DO ALL		B COMPUTEX		C SPEEDCOM		D SYMTEX				
			Info	Go/No Go	Info	Go/No Go	Info	Go/No Go	Info	Go/No Go			
• COMPATIBLE WITH LOGEX COMPUTER			LOGEX/BASEX	GO	LINKED/BASEX/GENTEX	GO	BASEX/GENTEX	NO GO	LOGEX	GO			
• COST LESS THAN $4000/MONTH			$3500/MONTH	GO	$3900/MONTH	GO	$3400/MONTH		$3600/MONTH	GO			
• INSTALLED BY JANUARY 1			DEC 15	GO	DEC.20+1WK.TEST	GO(?)	JAN.1		DEC.10	GO			
• OPERATOR TRAINING-MAXIMUM 5 DAYS			5 DAYS	GO	3 DAYS+2 DAYS LATER	GO	4 DAYS		2 DAYS	GO			

WANTS Include inverted *Musts*	Relative Weight		How well does each alternative perform against each *want?* Which one gets best score?										
			A DO ALL			B COMPUTEX			C SPEEDCOM			D SYMTEX		
			Info	Score	WT SC	Info	Score	WT SC	Info	Score	WT SC	Info	Score	WT SC
• CAPACITY TO PRODUCE ALL CURRENT REPORTS	10		• PRODUCTION SCH • SALES REPORTS • MAILING LISTS LATER	7	70	• PRODUCTION SCH • SALES REPORTS • MAILING LISTS NOW	10	100				• PRODUCTION SCH • SALES REPORTS	1	10
• INTER-UNIT COMMUNICATION	8		12 UNIT CAPABILITY	6	48	15 UNIT CAPABILITY	10	80				12 UNIT CAPABILITY	5	40
• EXPANSION CAPACITY	8		+50%	8	64	+60%	10	80				+40%	5	40
• GOOD SERVICING	7		DEALER NETWORK 80% COVERAGE	8	56	OWN NETWORK ENTIRE COUNTRY	10	70				AUTHORIZED DEALERS 25% COVERAGE	3	21
• MAXIMUM PRINTING SPEED	6		400 LINES/MINUTE	8	48	360 LINES/MINUTE PLUS OVERNIGHT	10	60				300 LINES/MINUTE	8	48
• BEST PRINTING QUALITY	5		JUSTIFIED MARGINS	5	25	JUSTIFIED MARGINS AUTOMATIC ERASING	10	50				JUSTIFIED MARGINS	5	25
• MINIMUM TRAINING TIME	4		NO TIME SAVINGS	8	32	NO TIME SAVINGS	6	24				3 DAYS GAINED	10	40
• AVAILABLE ASAP	2		DEC.15	8	16	DEC.31	5	10				DEC.10	10	20
• MINIMUM COST	1		$3500/MONTH	8	8	$3900/MONTH	5	5				$3600/MONTH	10	10
Total: index of performance					367			479						254

© Copyright, 1985, Decision Processes International. All rights reserved.

66

RISK EVALUATION

Situation 2
Select best word processor

RISKS	Degree of Risk Prob.	Ser.	Actions that could be taken to minimize the degree of risk	Residual Risk Prob.	Ser.
ALTERNATIVE: DO ALL **RISKS:**					
• SLOW SERVICE IN 20 % OF SITES	H	M			
• MAY NOT BE READY UNTIL DEC. 20	M	L			
ALTERNATIVE: COMPUTEX **RISKS:**	Prob.	Ser.			
• SLOW SERVICE-BRAND NEW NETWORK	H	H			
• COST OVERRUN	L	H			
• DELIVERY DELAYS-HAS OCCUR-RED IN 4 OF 5 CLIENTS SPOKEN TO	H	H			
ALTERNATIVE: **RISKS:**	Prob.	Ser.			

BEST BALANCED CHOICE: _____

67

DECISION ANALYSIS WORKSHEET

OBJECTIVE:

CRITERIA		ALTERNATIVES											
MUSTS < Minimum requirements Absolute constraints • Non-Negotiable • Limits • Measurable		Does each alternative meet each *must*?											
		A		B		C		D					
		Info	Go/No Go	Info	Go/No Go	Info	Go/No Go	Info	Go/No Go				

WANTS	Include inverted *Musts*	Relative Weight	How well does each alternative perform against each *want?* Which one gets best score?										
			Info	Score	WT SC	Info	Score	WT SC	Info	Score	WT SC	Info	Score	WT SC

Total: index of performance

RISK EVALUATION

ALTERNATIVE: RISKS:	Degree of Risk		Actions that could be taken to minimize the degree of risk	Residual Risk	
	Prob.	Ser.		Prob.	Ser.
ALTERNATIVE: RISKS:	Prob.	Ser.		Prob.	Ser.
ALTERNATIVE: RISKS:	Prob.	Ser.		Prob.	Ser.

BEST BALANCED CHOICE: _____

_____

POTENTIAL PROBLEM ANALYSIS

Let us now situate ourselves mentally in the future. Obviously, we want the future to be successful for us; this is why we need the Potential Problem Analysis (PPA). Potential Problem Analysis comes into play to implement the decision we have made in the previous step. The *logic path of Potential Problem Analysis* is as follows:

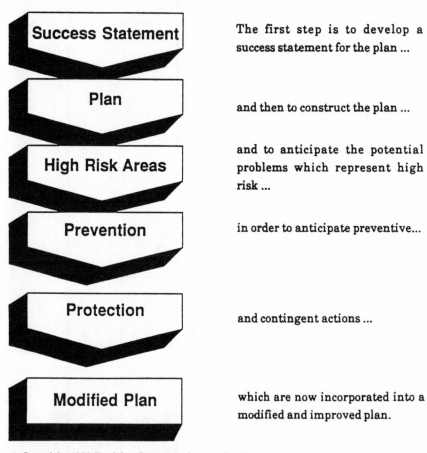

Success Statement

The first step is to develop a success statement for the plan ...

Plan

and then to construct the plan ...

High Risk Areas

and to anticipate the potential problems which represent high risk ...

Prevention

in order to anticipate preventive...

Protection

and contingent actions ...

Modified Plan

which are now incorporated into a modified and improved plan.

© Copyright 1988 Decision Processes International.
All rights reserved.

Success Statement

The principle of Potential Problem Analysis is to help us successfully implement a chosen course of action. We begin with a success statement.

The Plan

Our next step is to develop a plan and list its steps in chronological order. At this stage it is important to identify the steps that are of critical important to the plan's success.

High-Risk Areas

We identify the high-risk areas by examining the critical areas of the plan for potential problems. The amount of risk is then identified by looking at the probability and seriousness of each potential problem.

Prevention

Prevention is next. We can take preventive actions that are directed at the high-probability causes. We try to anticipate the likely causes of each potential problem together with the probability of each occurring. Preventive actions reduce the probability of a problem occurring and are taken in advance of the problem happening.

Protection

If our preventive actions fail and the potential problems materialize, we will need actions to protect us against the seriousness of the effects of the problem. These are called contingent actions because they come into play after the problem has occurred.

Modified Plan

The last step of Potential Problem Analysis is to take our original plan and to modify it by inserting, at the appropriate steps, the best selection of preventive and contingent actions. These should reduce the potential risk to a level that is acceptable. The modified plan is the one to implement because it has a higher probability of succeeding than the original one.

POTENTIAL PROBLEM ANALYSIS

LOGIC PATH

SUCCESS STATEMENT

PLAN

HIGH RISK AREAS

PREVENTION

PROTECTION

MODIFIED PLAN

PROCESS QUESTIONS

- What will be considered "success" in this situation?

- What are the activities, in chronological order, that will lead to success?

- What are the high risks areas?
- What is the probability and seriousness of each risk?

- What could cause these risks to occur?
- What actions can we take to prevent these potential obstacles?

- What actions can we think of to minimize the possible effects, should these problems occur?

- How should we modify our original plan?

POTENTIAL PROBLEM ANALYSIS WORKSHEET

SUCCESS STATEMENT:

PLAN STEPS	DATE	POTENTIAL PROBLEMS	RISKS PR.,SER	LIKELY CAUSES	PR.	PREVENTIVE ACTIONS	CONTINGENT ACTIONS	MODIFIED PLAN

SUMMARY

The questions of Situation Analysis are:

- What issues must be addressed or resolved?
- Is each issue so complex or so broad that it must be broken into discrete components?
- What is the priority of each issue or component in terms of seriousness, urgency, or growth?
- Which process is required for resolution—PA, DA, or PPA?

The questions of Problem Analysis are:

- What is the deviation?
- What/where/when and how much *is* the problem?
- What/where/when and how much *is not* the problem?
- What is different between the problem area and the nonproblem area?
- What changes have occurred in those differences?
- What are the possible causes?
- How do they test against our description of the problem?
- Which is the most probable cause?
- How was it verified?
- What action is recommended?

The questions of Decision Analysis are:

- What is the purpose of this decision?
- What are the *musts* and *wants*?
- What are the alternatives?
- How do the alternatives measure up to the *musts* and *wants*?
- What are the risks?
- What is the degree of risk?
- What is the best balanced choice?

Finally, the questions of Potential Problem Analysis are:

- What will be considered "success" in this situation?
- What are the steps of the plan?
- What are the high risks?
- What could cause these risks to occur?
- What preventive actions can we take?
- What contingent actions do we have?
- How will the plan be modified?

6

The Leader as Process Manager

One of the interesting misconceptions that senior executives have about their job descriptions revolves around what it is they think that they manage. During my twenty years of consulting work with senior executives, I have often asked them: "What do you, as managers, 'manage'?" Their answer, 99 percent of the time, is "people."

"Not so," say I!
"Oh?" they reply.
"That's right!" I reaffirm.
"What then?" they ask.
"Here's what people in organizations really manage," I reply.

Middle managers manage *people*. Senior managers manage *processes*. Lower level people manage *things*. In fact, one could view the hierarchy of management responsibility as follows:

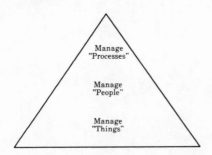

PEOPLE WHO MANAGE THINGS

These people are found at the bottom of the organization chart. They are the operators, mechanics, pipefitters, and electricians found in a manufacturing company, or the clerks and administrative personnel found in a white-collar area or in service industries. These people manage things. Their role is to get things done, to get the product out the door. Operators manage tools and production machines. Administrative people manage calculators, computers, or automatic teller machines (ATMs). They attempt to maintain these things in good working order in order to obtain the best yield and productivity from them.

PEOPLE WHO MANAGE PEOPLE

These individuals are found in the middle of the pyramid. They are usually referred to as supervisors, foremen, superintendents in a manufacturing environment, or section heads, department chiefs, or even directors in a white-collar environment. They manage people because it is their role to schedule employees' time and shifts of work, handle their work loads, resolve their conflicts, and ensure that they are generally happy in their work. These middle managers are concerned about logistics, scheduling, and relationships.

PEOPLE WHO MANAGE PROCESSES

These people reside at the zenith of the organization. Contrary to popular belief, these senior managers are not responsible for managing other people, but rather for managing processes. Senior executives are responsible for choosing and putting into place the processes, systems, and/or methods that will get the people in an organization to behave as the organization wants. These systems include:

• Compensation,

• Planning,

• Budgeting,

• Product development,

• Test marketing,

• Audit,

• Promotion,

• Performance review, and

• Job classification.

I have often said to clients: "If you want to change the behavior of people, put it into the "system."

To this list of "paper systems," our contention at DPI is that it is also management's responsibility to choose and put into place the *thinking processes* that they wish used in the organization. These are the processes of:

- Strategic thinking,
- Innovative thinking, and
- Decision making.

As I consult in various organizations, I am always told by the people of these organizations that "We have a different culture."

"What is your culture?" I ask.

"We cannot describe it," they reply, "but our culture is different than our competitors' or that of the company next door."

As a result of having heard these statements so frequently, I decided to investigate what it is about an organization that is at the root of that organization's culture. Studying organizations to uncover the answer to this mystery proved to be a futile exercise. To obtain an answer, we need instead to investigate what is at the root of the culture of a country. Then the answer becomes evident. The root of a country's culture is that country's language. Language is the root of literature, poetry, song, opera, music, theater, humor—all the elements that make up a country's "culture."

The analogy is this: Language is to a country's culture what management processes are to an organization's culture. Culture is the result of the processes that management chooses and uses to manage the organization.

Therefore, if management wants to create a certain culture in the organization, it must choose the processes that will cause its people to behave in a manner that results in the desired culture. The culture of an organization is the result of the processes with which management chooses to manage the business. This is so because a process provides a *common* language that can be used to deal more effectively with business issues. Just as language is the root of a country's music, literature, and theater, so is a common thinking process the root of better decisions, strategies, and opportunities for an organization.

If management wishes to breed a culture of sound strategic thinking, it must, thus, choose the process of strategic thinking that it wants its people to use. If management wishes to breed an innovative culture, then it must choose the process of innovation it wants its people to use. In other words, management's role is to select the "languages" that it wishes its people to speak while conducting business on behalf of the organization.

Management's most important responsibility is to institutionalize these processes into the organization so that they become part and parcel of its fabric and culture. However, we have found that institutionalizing thinking processes into an organization is easier said than done.

If one were to flowchart a business, the diagram would look like this:

Every business or organization can be broken down into three main components:

• Every business takes certain raw materials (inputs)
• and converts these (processes)
• into a finished product (output).

Furthermore, everyone would agree that the quality and quantity of the output is dependent on the effectiveness of the process to convert the input into a finished product. In fact, the quality and quantity of the finished product is determined by the effectiveness of the process.

However, there are two kinds of processes in existence in any business—tangible and intangible processes. The tangible processes are the obvious ones such as manufacturing, accounting, compensation and capital expenditure.

TANGIBLE PROCESSES

| Input (Raw Material) | Manufacturing / Invoicing / Recruiting / Marketing | Output (Product) |

The intangible processes are more subtle in nature but equally as important. These are the thinking processes that people use to manage the business, and are the processes we have been discussing in this book.

INTANGIBLE PROCESSES

Input (Data)	Strategic Thinking	Output (Results)
	Innovative Thinking	
	Decision Making	

In business today, most executives are investing enormous amounts of money to improve their tangible processes and relatively nothing to improve the intangible ones. Our view is that the war will be won by the organizations who can outthink their competitors rather than those who can "outmuscle" them.

The difficulty lies in the fact that we are not dealing with a visible system such as a compensation scheme but rather with an invisible process that occurs inside someone's head. The trick is to turn this invisible, uncoded, "soft" process into a codified, tangible tool that can be seen in "hard copy" form. As long as an organization's processes are uncodified and invisible, it will be difficult to perpetuate them and transmit them to other people. If an organization wants to be successful, it must codify its key thinking processes in order to transfer them to large groups of people and ensure their use on an ongoing basis. Process implementation, then, becomes a critical subject, and will be discussed in the following chapter.

"How many such processes should we try to indoctrinate into our people?" you might ask. The answer is simple. Just as the best linguists can usually master only four or five languages, the same is true about management, or thinking, processes. No organization should attempt to use more than a few management processes if it expects its people to use and master them over time. The task of choosing thinking processes that are *critical* to the success of the organization is a key task of senior management.

7

The Leader as Process Implementor

As a result of the work we have done in hundreds of companies in dozens of industries worldwide, the processes described in the previous chapters have been validated. In other words—they work. When properly used, they lead to faster and better decisions and conclusions.

However, what we have also noticed is that whether they work in your organization is not a function of the validity of the concepts but rather a function of the *implementation strategy* you use to bring the processes in-house. How you bring in these concepts and transmit them to your people is directly related to the results you will achieve. You can obtain very good results, very poor results, or anything in between.

In fact, the scope of possible implementation strategies and their accompanying results can be put onto a continuum such as the one that follows.

| Awareness | Individual
Skill
Building | Group
Process | Institutionali-
zation |

AWARENESS

This is the first strategy and the one that will produce the worst results. Unfortunately it is the one used by most organizations. Some wise man once explained that humanity goes through four stages of learning in life. These are:

- Unconscious incompetent,
- Conscious incompetent,
- Unconscious competent, and
- Conscious competent.

The unconscious incompetent is the person who is not very good at what he or she does but is not cognizant of the lack of competence. Such a person cannot be helped. The conscious incompetent is a person who is not skilled at what he or she does but is at least cognizant of that fact. Such a person will be receptive to help.

The unconscious competent is a person who is good at what he or she does but, unfortunately, does not understand why. Such persons cannot transfer their skill to anyone else since they do not understand it themselves. As mentioned before, some of the very best athletes never become good coaches because they never took the time to study why they were good and, therefore, cannot transfer their know-how to others. The conscious competent is in the best position to attain. This is a person who excels at what he or she does and is also cognizant of the method or process that he or she has perfected to attain that level of skill. Such a person can now transfer his or her knowledge to someone else. As mentioned earlier, this includes athletes who were "students of the game" and analyzed the process of winning so that they could transfer the formula to others and make them more competent.

As you probably have realized by now, most managers are in the third mode—that of the unconscious competent. In other words, most managers are reasonably competent but do not understand the root or cause of their competence. They are not aware of the processes they have mastered that creates their success. As such, they cannot transfer their skill to anyone else.

The awareness strategy, therefore, is to make these managers aware and cognizant of these processes. The technique to achieve this is very simple. You call these people together for two to three hours and you give them an overview of the concepts in visual form. You use tools such as overheads, posters, and flip charts that allow these people to see the concepts visually—in hard copy.

I call these sessions "ah-ah" sessions. As these managers see the processes come to life in hard copy form, they nod their heads up and down while murmuring in unison, "Ah-ah, ah-ah, ah-ah." The result is a lot of "ah-ah's" but no skill. Two or three hours is not enough time to build skill. We may have people cross the line and make these managers "aware" that there are processes of thinking that can be applied to business issues, but no skill can be developed around these processes in such a short period of time. Thus, we must move on to the next implementation strategy.

INDIVIDUAL SKILL BUILDING

The second possible implementation strategy is known as individual skill building. Its objective is to identify certain individuals whom management feels require help in these skills and send them to a training program of a longer duration, usually two or three days. The hope is that the person will come back as a "born-again" thinker, and that a dramatic improvement in decision-making ability will immediately occur. Unfortunately, there are several potential problems with this approach.

- First, the individual will see "being sent" to an outside course as indicating that he or she is in need of remedial treatment. "What's wrong with me?" will be that person's reaction.
- Second, the individual will return to the workplace with the full intention of using the concepts. Unfortunately, when he or she attempts to do so, he or she will find that others who do not understand the concepts and lack the patience to learn them. After a few futile attempts, our born-again "process convert" will simply give up and revert to his or her former habits.
- Third, by doing this to a large number of people, you end up frustrating rather than motivating the individuals involved.

For these reasons, although this second approach is better than the first, most companies abandon and move on to the next strategy.

GROUP PROCESS

This third strategy has a higher probability of producing better and longer-lasting results. Its objective is to identify groups of people who work together on a daily basis and provide them with a common process to address and resolve the issues they face in the course of their work.

Naturally, the first group that must learn and use these concepts is the top group—management. Experience has demonstrated to us that subordinates do what they see their bosses doing. If a superior is seen to be a practitioner and promoter of a certain process, then everyone will worship at the same altar. If the superior is not seen as being a practitioner of that process, no one will go to church. Even though you may have invested significant sums of money in the training of hundreds or even thousands of people in the lower levels of the organization, it will not be used. Save your money. If a process is perceived as not being good enough for management, it will then be perceived as valueless to anyone else. Therefore, management must start the ball rolling by being trained in these concepts itself and then becoming practitioners, sponsors, and promoters of the process. They must "take ownership" of the process.

Once this step has been achieved, the process can be cascaded down the organization. People are then brought to work sessions in homogeneous work groups, are introduced to the concepts, and then are given the opportunity to use the concepts in natural work teams on work-related issues that they share. Not surprisingly, they will make significant progress on these issues while in the room. In fact, they will probably make more progress than if they were sitting at their desks.

The other requirement of this strategy is that the work sessions be conducted by internal facilitators trained by us in advance. These facilitators, over time, play two important roles: First, they are trained as instructors in order to conduct the work sessions and introduce the people to the processes. A second, and more important role, however, is the one they play after the initial work sessions. Most people do not master new concepts or processes in two or three days. Instead, they need access to someone who can provide additional help on the spur of the moment when they attempt to use the concepts but may not understand them fully. These internal facilitators can provide further counsel and assistance to the group and help it use the concepts successfully. Success breeds a desire to use the process again and again.

These internal facilitators become an invaluable asset to the organization as "process consultants." Being selected to play this role for a period of time also provides tremendous personal development, and many of the facilitators will become good candidates for higher-level positions.

The thrust of this strategy is to cascade the process down the organization in "vertical slices" in order to achieve "critical mass" in that part of the company as quickly as possible. The rationale is simple: The more people there are in an organization who understand and share a common language, or process, the higher the probability that the process will be used on a consistent and continuous basis. The role of management in this strategy is to make the work environment conducive to the use of the process.

INSTITUTIONALIZATION

As can be deducted by its very name, this strategy is for the fanatics. This approach is for those managers who think that rational thinking is so powerful that their people should use it three times a day. Before you assume that the world would become dull if everyone became rational, please remind yourself that we are talking about the ability of an organization to succeed in a very competitive environment in which the difference between success and failure, profit and loss, and winning and losing means being just a little bit smarter than the other organization. Basically, it comes down to having a slightly better "batting average" than your competitor. In such surroundings, doing everything you can to make your people think more logically as often as possible is well worth the investment and may produce the marginal edge you need for success.

The strategy is simple: Over time, you incorporate into the systems and procedures used in the organization bits and pieces of the concepts and processes. This forces the use of the processes since people are obliged to use them each time they have to use a particular system. After a period of time and several such repetitive uses of the system, the use of the process will become reflex and routine.

There are many systems already in existence in any organization into which our concepts can be integrated. For example, the concepts of Problem Analysis can be built into customer complaint reports and maintenance work orders. The concepts of Decision Analysis can be incorporated into personnel selection and recruitment forms as well as capital expenditure requests. The concepts of our Innovation Process can be used in product development systems and test marketing programs. There are many other systems and procedures that exist in all organizations into which these concepts can be incorporated in order to encourage their use on an ongoing basis.

As I tell our clients: "If you want to change the behavior of your people, build it into the system!" Nothing works better.

IMPLEMENTATION STRATEGY

The implementation process is a reflection of the strategy.

Strategy	Methodology
Awareness	Process overview and information session.
Individual skill development	Individuals selected to attend a program with other individuals in heterogeneous groups (open workshops).
Group skill development	Homogeneous work groups are identified and attend an internal program. Important work issues are preidentified. Structured follow-up for optimum application.
Institutionalization of concepts and application	Individual/group skills developed as above. Deliberate introduction of key ideas into forms, systems, and procedures.

IMPLEMENTATION STRATEGY

OBJECTIVE: AWARENESS	INDIVIDUAL SKILL BUILDING	GROUP PROCESS	INSTITUTIONALIZATION

ACTIONS
- 2/3 HOUR OVERVIEW & INFORMATION SESSION

- PUBLIC SESSION
- INTER-COMPANY
- INTERNAL
- PUBLIC SESSION
- DPI-RUN

- INTERNAL FACILITATORS
- PRE-IDENTIFIED ISSUES
- VERTICAL SLICE
- HOMOGENEOUS GROUPS
- FOLLOW-UP & MAINTENANCE

- GRADUAL INTRODUCTION OF BITS/PIECES OF CONCEPTS INTO FORMS & SYSTEMS

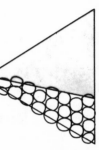
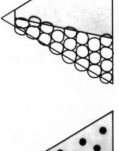

KEY ELEMENTS
- MANAGEMENT COMMITMENT, INVOLVEMENT & SUPPORT
- CRITICAL MASS
- USER OWNERSHIP

GROUP PROCESS STRATEGY

A SYSTEMATIC IMPLEMENTATION PLAN = BEST RESULTS

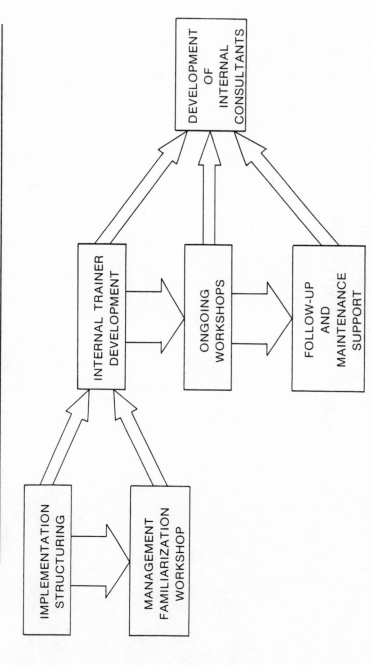

PROCESS EMPHASIS

EMPHASIS CHANGES WITH LEVEL OF MANAGEMENT

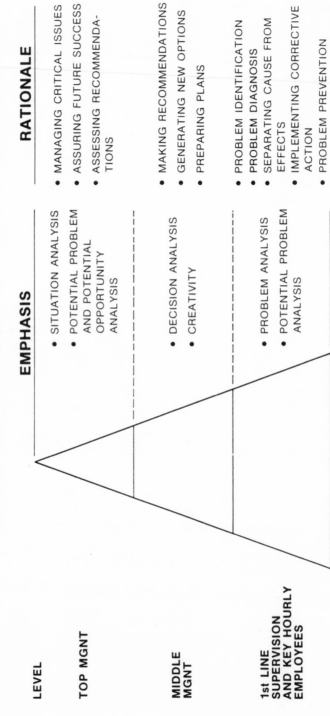

LEVEL	EMPHASIS	RATIONALE
TOP MGNT	• SITUATION ANALYSIS • POTENTIAL PROBLEM AND POTENTIAL OPPORTUNITY ANALYSIS	• MANAGING CRITICAL ISSUES • ASSURING FUTURE SUCCESS • ASSESSING RECOMMENDA-TIONS
MIDDLE MGNT	• DECISION ANALYSIS • CREATIVITY	• MAKING RECOMMENDATIONS • GENERATING NEW OPTIONS • PREPARING PLANS
1st LINE SUPERVISION AND KEY HOURLY EMPLOYEES	• PROBLEM ANALYSIS • POTENTIAL PROBLEM ANALYSIS	• PROBLEM IDENTIFICATION • PROBLEM DIAGNOSIS • SEPARATING CAUSE FROM EFFECTS • IMPLEMENTING CORRECTIVE ACTION • PROBLEM PREVENTION

GROUP PROCESS STRATEGY

There are three critical elements for successful implementation of decision-making processes into an organization.

1. Management commitment, involvement, and support,
2. A critical mass of people who have learned and apply the process in homogeneous work groups, and
3. Ongoing application of the process on real situations (internal consulting help should be available).

Proposed General Implementation Plan

Phase	Element	Key Activities
I	Implementation structuring	Overview orientation meeting; Population identification; Objectives and key issues identified; and Selection of implementation coordinator.
II	Management familiarization workshop	Executive management workshop (two to three days).
III	Internal trainers' development	Selection of instructor candidates; Instructor training program; First program observation and support; and Ongoing coaching and support.
IV	Ongoing schedule of workshops	Scheduling of workshops and participants; Coordination of facilities, materials, and trainers; Identification of issues/participants; and Evaluation
V	Development of internal consultants	Selection of proposed process facilitators/consultants; Consulting skills development; and Ongoing coaching and support.

Implementation Involves a Variety of Important Roles

Senior management	Visible sponsor and user; Encourage application; Make people available for workshops; and Ensure adequate budget.
Program Coordinator	Coordinates execution of workshop schedule; Monitors instructors' effectiveness; and Ensures adequate follow-up and maintenance.
Program instructor	Workshop leader; Coaches participants concerning application; and Modifies presentation to suit audience.

Process consultant   Process leader on specific issues; Process
                                                advisor to working groups; and Process
                                                coach to managers/others.

DPI   Assist with structuring; Development of
                                                internal resources; Supplier of materials
                                                and methodology; Provide on-going
                                                support/evaluation and counsel; and
                                                External process consultant.

8

Building Learning Organizations*
PETER M. SENGE

Human beings are designed for learning. No one has to teach an infant to walk, or talk, or master the spatial relationships needed to stack eight building blocks so they do not topple. Children come fully equipped with an insatiable drive to explore and experiment. Unfortunately, the primary institutions of our society are oriented predominantly toward controlling rather than learning, rewarding individuals for performing for others rather than for cultivating their natural curiosity and impulse to learn. The young child entering school discovers quickly that the name of the game is getting the right answer and avoiding mistakes—a mandate no less compelling to the aspiring manager.

"Our prevailing system of management has destroyed our people," writes W. Edwards Deming, a leader in the quality movement.

People are born with intrinsic motivation, self-esteem, dignity, curiosity to learn, joy in learning. The forces of destruction begin with toddlers—a prize for the best Halloween costume, grades in school, gold stars, and on up through the university. On the job, people, teams, divisions are ranked—reward for the one at the top, punishment at the bottom. MBO [Management by Objectives], quotas, incentive pay, business plans, put together separately, division by division, cause further loss, unknown and unknowable.[1]

Ironically, by focusing on performing for someone else's approval, corporations create the very conditions that predestine them to mediocre

*This chapter is reprinted from "The Leaders' New Work" by Peter M. Senge, *Sloan Management Review* (Fall 1990), by permission of the publisher. Copyright 1990 by the Sloan Management Review Association. All rights reserved.

performance. Over the long run, superior performance depends on superior learning. A Shell study showed that, according to former planning director Arie de Geus, "a full one-third of the Fortune '500' industrials listed in 1970 had vanished by 1983."[2] Today, the average lifetime of the largest industrial enterprises is probably less than half the average lifetime of a person in an industrial society. On the other hand, de Geus and his colleagues at Shell also found a small number of companies that had survived for seventy-five years or longer. Interestingly, the key to their survival was the ability to run "experiments in the margin," to continually explore new business and organizational opportunities that create potential new sources of growth.

If anything, the need for understanding how organizations learn and accelerating that learning is greater today than ever before. The old days when a Henry Ford, Alfred Sloan, or Tom Watson *learned for* the organization are gone. In an increasingly dynamic, interdependent, and unpredictable world, it is simply no longer possible for anyone to "figure it all out at the top." The old model of "the top thinks and the local acts" must now give way to integrating thinking and acting at all levels. While the challenge is great, so is the potential payoff. "The person who figures out how to harness the collective genius of the people in his or her organization," according to former Citibank CEO Walter Wriston, "is going to blow the competition away."[3]

ADAPTIVE LEARNING AND GENERATIVE LEARNING

The prevailing view of learning organizations emphasizes increased adaptability. Given the accelerating pace of change, or so the standard view goes, "the most successful corporation of the 1990s," according to B. Domain in *Fortune* magazine, "will be something called a learning organization, a consummately adaptive enterprise."[4] As the Shell study shows, examples of traditional authoritarian bureaucracies that responded too slowly to survive in changing business environments are legion.

However, increasing adaptiveness is only the first stage in moving toward learning organizations. The impulse to learn in children goes deeper than desires to respond and adapts more effectively to environmental change. The impulse to learn, at its heart, is an impulse to be generative, to expand our capability. This is why leading corporations are focusing on *generative* learning, which concerns creating, as well as *adaptive* learning, which concerns coping.[5]

The total quality movement in Japan illustrates the evolution from adaptive to generative learning. With its emphasis on continuous experimentation and feedback, the total quality movement has been the first wave in building learning organizations. However, the Japanese firms' view of serving the customer has evolved. In the early years of total quality, the focus was on "fitness to standard," making a product reliably so that it would do what its designers intended it to do and what the firm told its customers it would do. Then came a focus on "fitness to need," understanding better what the customer wanted and then providing products that reliably met those needs. Today, leading-edge firms seek to understand and meet the "latent need" of the customer—what the customer might truly value but has never experienced or would never think to ask for. As one Detroit executive commented recently, "You could never produce the Mazda Miata solely from market research. It required a leap of imagination to see what the customer *might* want."

Generative learning, unlike adaptive learning, requires new ways of looking at the world, whether in understanding customers or in understanding how to better manage a business. For years, U.S. manufacturers sought competitive advantage through aggressive controls on inventories, incentives against overproduction, and rigid adherence to production forecasts. Despite these incentives, their performance was eventually eclipsed by Japanese firms which saw the challenges of manufacturing differently. They realized that eliminating delays in the production process was the key to reducing instability and improving cost, productivity, and service. They worked to build networks of relationships with trusted suppliers and to redesign physical production processes so as to reduce delays in materials procurement, production setup, and in-process inventory—a much higher-leverage approach to improving both cost and customer loyalty.

As Boston Consulting Group's George Stalk has observed, the Japanese saw the significance of delays because they saw the process of order entry, production scheduling, materials procurement, production, and distribution as an integrated system. "What distorts the system so badly is time," observed Stalk—the multiple delays between events and responses. "These distortions reverberate throughout the system, producing disruptions, waste, and inefficiency."[6] Generative learning requires seeing the systems that control events. When we fail to grasp the systemic source of problems, we are left to "push on" symptoms rather than eliminating underlying causes. The best we can ever do in that case is adaptive learning.

THE LEADER'S NEW WORK

"I talk with people all over the country about learning organizations, and the response is always very positive," says William O'Brien, CEO of the Hanover Insurance Companies. "If this type of organization is so widely preferred, why don't people create such organizations? I think the answer is leadership. People have no real comprehension of the type of commitment it requires to build such an organization."[7]

Our traditional view of leaders—as special people who set the direction, make the key decisions, and energize the troops—is deeply rooted in an individualistic and nonsystemic worldview. Especially in the West, leaders are heroes—great men (and occasionally women) who rise to the fore in times of crisis. As long as such myths prevail, they reinforce a focus on short-term events and charismatic heroes rather than on systemic forces and collective learning.

Leadership in learning organizations centers on subtler and ultimately more important work. In a learning organization, leaders' roles differ dramatically from that of the charismatic decision maker. Leaders are designers, teachers, and stewards. These roles require new skills: the ability to build shared vision, to bring to the surface and challenge prevailing mental models, and to foster more systemic patterns of thinking. In short, leaders in learning organizations are responsible for *building organizations* in which people are continually expanding their capabilities to shape their future—that is, leaders are responsible for learning.

CREATIVE TENSION: THE INTEGRATING PRINCIPLE

Leadership in a learning organization starts with the principle of creative tension.[8] Creative tension comes from seeing clearly where we want to be—our "vision"—and telling the truth about where we are; that is, our "current reality." The gap between the two generates a natural tension.

Creative tension can be resolved in two basic ways: by raising current reality toward the vision, or by lowering the vision toward current reality. Individuals, groups, and organizations that learn how to work with creative tension learn how to use the energy it generates to move reality more reliably toward their visions.

The principle of creative tension has long been recognized by leaders. Martin Luther King, Jr., once said:

Just as Socrates felt that it was necessary to create a tension in the mind, so that individuals could rise from the bondage of myths and half truths . . . so must we . . . create the kind of tension in society that will help men rise from the dark depths of prejudice and racism.[9]

Without vision there is no creative tension. Creative tension cannot be generated from current reality alone. All the analysis in the world will never generate a vision. Many who are otherwise qualified to lead fail to do so because they try to substitute analysis for vision. They believe that if people only understood current reality, they would surely feel the motivation to change. They are then disappointed to discover that people "resist" the personal and organizational changes that must be made to alter reality. What they never grasp is that the natural energy for changing reality comes from holding a picture of what might be that is more important to people than what is.

However, creative tension cannot be generated from vision alone; it demands an accurate picture of current reality as well. Just as King had a dream, so too did he continually strive to "dramatize the shameful conditions" of racism and prejudice so that they could no longer be ignored. Vision without an understanding of current reality will more likely foster cynicism than creativity. The principle of creative tension teaches that an accurate picture of current reality is just as important as a compelling picture of a desired future.

Leading through creative tension is different than solving problems. In problem solving, the energy for change comes from attempting to get away from an aspect of current reality that is undesirable. With creative tension, the energy for change comes from the vision—from what we want to create—juxtaposed with current reality. While the distinction may seem small, the consequences are not. Many people and organizations find themselves motivated to change only when their problems are bad enough to cause them to change. This works for a while, but the change process will run out of steam as soon as the problems driving the change become less pressing. With problem solving, the motivation for change is extrinsic, while with creative tension, the motivation is intrinsic. This distinction mirrors the distinction between adaptive and generative learning.

NEW ROLES

The traditional authoritarian image of the leader as "the boss calling the shots" has been recognized as oversimplified and inadequate for some time. According to Edgar Schein, "Leadership is intertwined with culture formation." Building an organization's culture and shaping its evolution is the "unique and essential function" of leadership.[10] In a learning organization, the critical roles of leadership—designer, teacher, and steward—have antecedents in the ways in which leaders have contributed to building organizations in the past. However, each role takes on new meaning in the learning organization, and demands new skills and tools.

The Leader as Designer

Imagine that your organization is an ocean liner and that you are "the leader." What is your role?

I have asked this question of groups of managers many times. The most common answer, not surprisingly, is "The captain." Others say, "The navigator, setting the direction." Still others say, "The helmsman, actually controlling the direction"; "The engineer down there stoking the fire, providing energy"; or "The social director, making sure everybody's enrolled, involved, and communicating." While these are legitimate leadership roles, there is another that, in many ways, eclipses them all in importance, yet rarely does anyone mention it.

The neglected leadership role is the *designer* of the ship. No one has a more sweeping influence than the designer. What good does it do for the captain to say, "Turn starboard 30 degrees," when the designer has built a rudder that will only turn to port or that takes six hours to turn to starboard? It is fruitless to be the leader in an organization that is poorly designed.

The functions of design, or what some have called "social architecture," are rarely visible; they take place behind the scenes. The consequences that appear today are the result of work done long in the past, and work today will show its benefits far in the future. Those who aspire to lead out of a desire to control, or gain fame, or simply to be at the center of the action, will find little to attract them to the quiet design work of leadership.

What, specifically, is involved in organizational design? "Organization design is widely misconstrued as moving around boxes and lines," says Hanover's O'Brien. "The first task of organization design concerns designing the governing ideas of purpose, vision, and core values by which people will live." Few acts of leadership have a more enduring impact on an organization than building a foundation of purpose and core values.

In 1982, Johnson & Johnson found itself facing a corporate nightmare when bottles of its best-selling product Tylenol were tampered with, resulting in several deaths. The corporation's immediate response was to pull all Tylenol off the shelves of retail outlets. Thirty-one million capsules were destroyed, even though they were tested and found safe. Although the immediate cost was significant, no other action was possible given the firm's credo. Authored almost forty years earlier by president Robert Wood Johnson, Johnson & Johnson's credo states that permanent success is possible only when modern industry realizes that:

- Service to its customers comes first;
- Service to its employees and management comes second;
- Service to the community comes third; and
- Service to its stockholders comes last.

Such statements might seem like "motherhood and apple pie" to those who have not seen the way in which a clear sense of purpose and values can affect key business decisions. Johnson & Johnson's crisis management in this case was based on that credo. It was simple, it was right, and it worked.

If governing ideas constitute the first design task of leadership, the second design task involves the policies, strategies, and structures that translate guiding ideas into business decisions. Leadership theorist Philip Selznick calls policy and structure the "institutional embodiment of purpose."[11] "Policy making (the rules that guide decisions) ought to be separated from decision making," says Jay Forrester.[12] "Otherwise, short-term pressures will usurp time from policy creation."

Traditionally, writers like Selznick and Forrester have tended to see policy-making and implementation as the work of a small number of senior managers. However, that view is changing. Both the dynamic business environment and the mandate of the learning organization to engage people at all levels now make it clear that this second design task is more subtle. Henry Mintzberg has argued that strategy is less a rational plan arrived at in the abstract and implemented throughout the organization than an "emergent phenomenon." Successful organizations "craft strategy," according to Mintzberg, as they continually learn about shifting business conditions and balance what is desired and what is possible.[13] The key is not getting the right strategy but fostering strategic thinking. "The choice of individual action is only part of . . . the policymaker's need," according to R. Mason and I. Mitroff. "More important is the need to achieve insight into the nature of the complexity and to formulate concepts and world views for coping with it."[14]

Behind appropriate policies, strategies, and structures are effective learning processes; their creation is the third key design responsibility in learning organizations. This does not absolve senior managers of their strategic responsibilities. Instead, they become responsible not only for ensuring that an organization has well-developed strategies and policies but also for ensuring that processes exist whereby these are continually improved.

In the early 1970s, Shell was the weakest of the big seven U.S. oil companies. Today, Shell and Exxon are arguably the strongest, both in size and financial health. Shell's ascendance began with frustration. Around 1971 members of Shell's Group Planning Division in London began to foresee dramatic change and unpredictability in world oil markets. However, it proved impossible to persuade managers that the stable world of steady growth in oil demand and supply that they had known for twenty years was about to change. Despite brilliant analysis and artful presentation, Shell's planners realized, in the words of Pierre Wack, that they "had failed to change behavior in much of the Shell organization."[15] Progress would probably have ended there had the frustration not given way to a radically new view of corporate planning.

As they pondered this failure, the planners' view of their basic task shifted: "We no longer saw our task as producing a documented view of the future business environment five or ten years ahead. Our real target was the microcosm (the 'mental model') of our decision makers." Only when the planners reconceptualized their basic task as fostering learning rather than devising plans did their insights begin to have an impact. The initial tool used was "scenario analysis," through which planners encouraged operating managers to think through how they would manage in the future under different possible scenarios. It mattered not that the managers believe the planners' scenarios absolutely, only that they become engaged in ferreting out the implications. In this way, Shell's planners conditioned managers to be mentally prepared for shifts from low prices to high prices and from stability to instability. The results were significant. When the Organization of Petroleum Exporting Companies (OPEC) became a reality, Shell quickly responded by increasing the control of local operating companies (to enhance maneuverability in the new political environment), building buffer stocks, and accelerating development of non-OPEC sources—actions that its competitors took either much more slowly or not at all.

Somewhat inadvertently, Shell planners had discovered the leverage of designing institutional learning processes, whereby, in the words of former planning director de Geus, "Management teams change their shared mental models of their company, their markets, and their competitors."[16] Since then, "planning as learning" has become a byword at Shell, and Group Planning has continually sought out new learning tools that can be integrated into the planning process. Some of these are described below.

The Leader as Teacher

"The first responsibility of a leader," writes retired Herman Miller CEO Max de Pree, "is to define reality."[17] Much of the leverage that leaders can actually exert lies in helping people achieve more accurate, more insightful, and more *empowering* views of reality.

Leader as teacher does not mean leader as authoritarian expert whose job it is to teach people the "correct" view of reality. Rather, it involves helping everyone in the organization, oneself included, to gain more insightful views of current reality. This is in line with a popular emerging view of leaders as coaches, guides, or facilitators.[18] In learning organizations, this teaching role is developed further by virtue of explicit attention to people's mental models and by the influence of the systems perspective.

The role of leader as teacher starts with bringing to the surface people's mental models of important issues. No one carries an organization, a market, or a state of technology in his or her head. What we do carry in our heads are assumptions. These mental pictures of how the world works have a significant influence on how we perceive problems and opportunities, identify courses of action, and make choices.

One reason that mental models are so deeply entrenched is that they are largely tacit. Ian Mitroff, in his study of General Motors, argues that an assumption that prevailed for years was that in the United States, "cars are status symbols. Styling is therefore more important than quality."[19] The Detroit automakers did not say, 'We have a *mental model* that all people care about is styling." Few actual managers would even say publicly that all that people care about is styling. As long as the view remained unexpressed, there was little possibility of challenging its validity or forming more accurate assumptions.

However, working with mental models goes beyond revealing hidden assumptions. "Reality," as perceived by most people in most organizations, means pressures that must be borne, crises that must be reacted to, and limitations that must be accepted. Leaders as teachers help people restructure their views of reality to see beyond the superficial conditions and events into the underlying causes of problems—and therefore to see new possibilities for shaping the future.

Specifically, leaders can influence people to view reality at three distinct levels: events, patterns of behavior, and systemic structure.

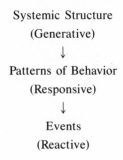

The key question becomes, "Where do leaders predominantly focus their own and their organization's attention?"

Contemporary society focuses predominantly on events. The media reinforces this perspective, with almost exclusive attention to short-term, dramatic events. This focus leads naturally to explaining what happens in terms of those events: "The Dow Jones average went up sixteen points because high fourth-quarter profits were announced yesterday."

Pattern-of-behavior explanations are rarer, in contemporary culture, than event explanations, but they do occur. "Trend analysis" is an example of seeing patterns of behavior. A good editorial that interprets a set of current events in the context of long-term historical changes is another example. Systemic, structural explanations go even further by addressing the question, "What causes the patterns of behavior?"

In some sense, all three levels of explanation are equally true. However, their usefulness is quite different. Event explanations—who did what to whom—doom their holders to a reactive stance toward change. Pattern-of-behavior explanations focus on identifying long-term trends and assessing their implications. They at least suggest how, over time, we can respond to shifting conditions. Structural explanations are the most powerful. Only they address the underlying causes of behavior at such a level that patterns of behavior can be changed.

By and large, leaders of our current institutions focus their attention on events and patterns of behavior, and, under their influence, their organizations do likewise. That is why contemporary organizations are predominantly reactive, or at best responsive—and rarely generative. On the other hand, leaders in learning organizations pay attention to all three levels, but focus especially on systemic structure; largely by example, they teach people throughout the organization to do likewise.

The Leader as Steward

This is the subtlest role of leadership. Unlike the roles of designer and teacher, it is almost solely a matter of attitude, an attitude that is critical to learning organizations.

While stewardship has long been recognized as an aspect of leadership, its source is still not widely understood. I believe Robert Greenleaf came closest to explaining real stewardship, in his seminal book *Servant Leadership*.[20] There, Greenleaf argues that:

The servant leader *is* servant first. . . . It begins with the natural feeling that one wants to serve, to serve *first*. This conscious choice brings one to aspire to lead. That person is sharply different from one who is leader first, perhaps because of the need to assuage an unusual power drive or to acquire material possessions.

Leaders' sense of stewardship operates on two levels: stewardship for the people they lead and stewardship for the larger purpose or mission that underlies the enterprise. The first type arises from a keen appreciation of the impact one's leadership can have on others. People can suffer economically, emotionally, and spiritually under inept leadership. If anything, people in a learning organization are more vulnerable because of their commitment and sense of shared ownership. Appreciating this naturally instills a sense of responsibility in leaders. The second type of stewardship arises from a leader's sense of personal purpose and commitment to the organization's larger mission. People's natural impulse to learn is unleashed when they are engaged in an endeavor that they consider worthy of their fullest commitment. As Lawrence Miller puts it:

Achieving return on equity does not, as a goal, mobilize the most noble forces of our soul. This is the true joy in life, the being used for a purpose you consider is a mighty one, the being a force of nature rather than a feverish, selfish clod of ailments and grievances complaining that the world will not devote itself to making you happy.[21]

NEW SKILLS

New leadership roles require new leadership skills. These skills can only be developed through a lifelong commitment. It is not enough for one or two individuals to develop these skills. They must be distributed widely throughout the organization. This is one reason why understanding the *disciplines* of a learning organization is so important. These disciplines embody the principles and practices that can widely foster leadership development.

Three critical areas of skills (disciplines) are building shared vision, surfacing and challenging mental models, and engaging in systems thinking.

Building Shared Vision

How do individual visions come together to create shared visions? A useful metaphor is the hologram, the three-dimensional image created by interacting light sources. If you cut a photograph in half, each half shows only part of the whole image. But if you divide a hologram, each part, no matter how small, shows the whole image intact. Likewise, when a group of people come to share a vision for an organization, each person sees an individual picture of the organization at its best. Each shares responsibility for the whole, not just for one piece. However, the component pieces of the hologram are not identical. Each represents the whole image from a different point of view. It is something like poking holes in a window shade; each hole offers a unique angle for viewing the whole image. So, too, is each individual's vision unique.

When you add up the pieces of a hologram, something interesting happens. The image becomes more intense and lifelike. When more people come to share a vision, the vision becomes more real in the sense of a mental reality that people can truly imagine achieving. They now have partners, cocreators; the vision no longer rests on their shoulders alone. Early on, when they are nurturing an individual vision, people may say it is "my vision." However, as the shared vision develops, it becomes both "my vision" and "our vision." The skills involved in building a shared vision include the following:

Encouraging Personal Vision. Shared visions emerge from personal visions. It is not that people only care about their own self-interest—in fact, people's values usually include dimensions that concern family, organization, community, and even the world. Rather, it is that people's capacity for caring is personal.

Communicating and Asking for Support. Leaders must be willing to continually share their own vision rather than being the official representative of the corporate vision. They also must be prepared to ask, "Is this vision worthy of your commitment?" This can be difficult for a person who is used to setting goals and presuming compliance.

Visioning as an Ongoing Process. Building shared vision is a never-ending process. At any one point there will be a particular image of the future that is predominant, but that image will evolve. Today, too many managers want to dispense with the "vision business" by going off and writing the official vision statement. Such statements almost always lack the vitality, freshness, and excitement of a genuine vision that comes from people asking, "What do we really want to achieve?"

Blending Extrinsic and Intrinsic Visions. Many energizing visions are extrinsic—that is, they focus on achieving something relative to an outsider, such as a competitor. However, a goal that is limited to defeating an opponent can, once the vision has been achieved, easily become a defensive posture. In contrast, intrinsic goals like creating a new type of product, taking an established product to a new level, or setting a new standard for customer satisfaction can call forth a new level of creativity and innovation. Intrinsic and extrinsic visions need to coexist; a vision solely predicated on defeating an adversary will eventually weaken an organization.

Distinguishing Positive from Negative Visions. Many organizations only truly pull together when their survival is threatened. Similarly, most social movements aim at eliminating what people do not want: for example, antidrugs, antismoking, or antinuclear arms movements. Negative visions carry a subtle message of powerlessness: People will only pull together when there is sufficient threat. Negative visions also tend to be short-term. Two fundamental sources of energy can motivate organizations: fear and aspiration. Fear, the energy source behind negative visions, can produce extraordinary changes in short periods, but aspiration endures as a continuing source of learning and growth.

Surfacing and Testing Mental Models

Many of the best ideas in organizations never are put into practice. One reason is that new insights and initiatives often conflict with established mental models. The leadership task of challenging assumptions without invoking defensiveness requires reflection and inquiry skills possessed by few leaders in traditional controlling organizations.

Seeing Leaps of Abstraction. Our minds literally move at lightning speed. Ironically, this often slows our learning because we leap to generalizations so quickly that we never think to test them. We then confuse our generalizations with the observable data on which they were based, treating the generalizations as if they were data. The frustrated sales representative (rep) reports to the home office that "customers don't really care about quality, price is what matters," when what actually happened was that three consecutive large customers refused to place an order unless a larger discount was offered. The sales rep treats here generalization that "customers care only about price," as if it were absolute fact rather than an assumption (and very likely an assumption reflecting her own views of customers and the market). This thwarts future learning because she starts to focus on how to offer attractive discounts rather than probing behind the customers' statements. For example, the customers may have been disgruntled with the firm's delivery or customer service and therefore became unwilling to purchase again without larger discounts.

Balancing Inquiry and Advocacy. Most managers are skilled at articulating their views and presenting them persuasively. While important, advocacy skills can become counterproductive as managers rise in responsibility and confront increasingly complex issues that require collaborative learning among different, equally knowledgeable people. Leaders in learning organizations need to have both inquiry and advocacy skills.

Specifically, when advocating a view, leaders must be able to:

—Explain the reasoning and data that led to their view;

—Encourage others to test their view (e.g., "Do you see gaps in my reasoning? Do you disagree with the data upon which my view is based?"); and

—Encourage others to provide different views (e.g., "Do you have either different data, different conclusions, or both?").

When inquiring into another's views, they need to:

—Actively seek to understand the other's view rather than simply restating their own view and the way in which it differs from the other's view; and

—Make their attributions about the other and the other's view explicitly (e.g., "Based on your statement that . . . ; I am assuming that you believe . . . ; Am I representing your views fairly?").

If they reach an impasse (others no longer appear open to inquiry), they need to:

—Ask what data or logic might unfreeze the impasse, or whether an experiment (or some other inquiry) might be designed to provide new information.

Distinguished Espoused Theory from Theory in Use. We all like to think that we hold certain views, but often our actions reveal deeper ones. For example, I may proclaim that people are trustworthy but never lend friends money and jealously guard my possessions. Obviously, my deeper mental model (my theory in use), differs from my espoused theory. Recognizing gaps between espoused views and theories in use (which often requires the help of others) can be pivotal to deeper learning.

Recognizing and Defusing Defensive Routines. As one CEO puts it, "Nobody ever talks about an issue at the 8:00 business meeting exactly the same way they talk about it at home that evening or over drinks at the end of the day." The reason is what Chris Argyris calls "defensive routines," entrenched habits used to protect ourselves from the embarrassment and threat that come with exposing our thinking. For most of us, such defenses began to build early in life in response to pressures to have the right answers in school or at home. Organizations add new levels of performance anxiety and thereby amplify and exacerbate this defensiveness. Ironically, this makes it even more difficult to expose hidden mental models, and it thereby lessens learning.

The first challenge is to recognize defensive routines, and then to inquire into their operation. Those who are best at revealing and defusing defensive routines operate with a high degree of self-disclosure regarding their own defensiveness (e.g., "I notice that I am feeling uneasy about how this conversation is going. Perhaps I don't understand it or it is threatening to me in ways I don't yet see. Can you help me see this better?")

Systems Thinking

We all know that leaders should help people see the big picture. However, the actual skills whereby leaders are supposed to achieve this are not well understood. In my experience, successful leaders often *are* systems thinkers to a considerable extent. They focus less on day-to-day events and more on underlying trends and forces of change. However, they do this almost completely intuitively. The consequence is that they are often unable to explain their intuitions to others and feel frustrated that others cannot see the world in the way that they do.

One of the most significant developments in management science today is the gradual coalescence of managerial systems thinking as a field of study and practice. This field suggests some key skills for future leaders:

Seeing Interrelationships, Not Things, and Processes, Not Snapshots. Most of us have been conditioned throughout our lives to focus on things and to see the world in static images. This leads us to linear explanations of systemic phenomenon. For instance, in an arms race, each nation is convinced that the other is the cause of problems. They react to each new move as an isolated event, not as part of a process. As long as they fail to see the interrelationships of these actions, they will be trapped.

Moving beyond Blame. We tend to blame each other or outside circumstances for our problems. However, it is poorly designed systems, not incompetent or unmotivated individuals, that cause most organizational problems. Systems thinking shows us that there is no "outside"—that you and the cause of your problems are part of a single system.

Distinguishing Detail Complexity from Dynamic Complexity. Some types of complexity are more important strategically than others. Detail complexity arises when there are many variables. Dynamic complexity arises when cause and effect are distant in time and space, and when the consequences over time of interventions are subtle and not obvious to many participants in the system. The leverage in most management situations lies in understanding dynamic complexity, not detail complexity.

Focusing on Areas of High Leverage. Some have called systems thinking the "new dismal science" because it teaches that most obvious solutions do not work—at best, they improve matters in the short run, only to make things worse in the long run. However, there is another side to the story. Systems thinking also shows that small, well-focused actions can produce significant, enduring improvements, if they are taken in the right place. Systems thinkers refer to this idea as the principle of leverage. Tackling a difficult problem is often a matter of seeing where the high leverage lies, where a change—with a minimum of effort—would lead to lasting, significant improvement.

Avoiding Symptomatic Solutions. The pressures to intervene in management systems that are going awry can be overwhelming. Unfortunately, given the linear thinking that predominates in most organizations, interventions usually focus on symptomatic fixes, not underlying causes. This results in only temporary relief, and it tends to create still more pressures later on for further, low-leverage intervention. If leaders acquiesce to these pressures, they can be sucked into an endless spiral of increasing intervention. Sometimes the most difficult leadership acts are to refrain from intervening through popular quick fixes and to keep the pressure on everyone to identify more enduring solutions.

While leaders who can articulate systemic explanations are rare, those who can do so will leave their stamp on an organization. One person who had this gift was Bill Gore, the founder and long-time CEO of W. L. Gore and Associates (makers of Gore-Tex and other synthetic fiber products). Bill Gore was adept at telling stories that showed how the organization's core values of freedom and individual responsibility required particular operating policies. He was proud of his egalitarian organization, in which there were (and still are) no "employees," only "associates," all of whom own shares in the company and participate in its management. At one talk, he explained the company's policy of controlled growth:

Our limitation is not financial resources. Our limitation is the rate at which we can bring in new associates. Our experience has been that if we try to bring in more than a 25 percent per year increase, we begin to bog down. Twenty-five percent per year growth is a real limitation; you can do much better than that with an authoritarian organization.

As Gore tells the story, one of the associates, Esther Baum, went home after this talk and reported the limitation to her husband. As it happened, he was an astronomer and mathematician at Lowell Observatory. He said, "That's a very interesting figure." He took out a pencil and paper and made some calculations. Then he said, "Do you realize that in only fifty-seven and a half years, everyone in the world will be working for Gore?"

Through this story, Gore explains the systemic rationale behind a key policy, limited growth rate—a policy that undoubtedly caused a lot of stress in the organization. He suggests that, at larger rates of growth, the adverse effects of attempting to integrate too many new people too rapidly would begin to dominate. (This is the "limits to growth" systems archetype, which will be explained below.) The story also reaffirms the organization's commitment to creating a unique environment for its associates and illustrates the types of sacrifices that the firm is prepared to make in order to remain true to its vision. The last part of the story shows that, despite the self-imposed limit, the company is still very much a growth company.

The consequences of leaders who lack systems thinking skills can be devastating. Many charismatic leaders manage almost exclusively at the level of events. They deal with visions and crises, and with little in between. Under their leadership, an organization hurtles from crisis to crisis. Eventually, the worldview of people in the organization becomes dominated by events and reactiveness. Many, especially those who are deeply committed, become "burned out." Eventually, cynicism comes to pervade the organization. People have no control over their time, let alone their destiny.

Similar problems arise with the "visionary strategist," the leader with vision who sees both patterns of change and events. This leader is better prepared to manage change. He or she can explain strategies in terms of emerging trends, and thereby foster a climate that is less reactive. However, such leaders still impart a responsive orientation rather than a generative one.

Many talented leaders have rich, highly systemic intuitions but cannot explain those intuitions to others. Ironically, they often end up being authoritarian leaders, even if they do not want to, because only they see the decisions that need to be made. They are unable to conceptualize their strategic insights so that these can become public knowledge, open to challenge and further improvement.

NEW TOOLS

Developing the skills described above requires new tools—tools that will enhance leaders' conceptual abilities and foster communication and collaborative inquiry. What follows is a sampling of the tools that are starting to find use in learning organizations.

Systems Archetypes

One of the insights of the budding field of managerial systems thinking is that certain types of systemic structures recur again and again. Countless systems grow for a period and then encounter problems and cease to grow (or even collapse) well before they have reached the intrinsic limits to growth. Many other systems get locked in runaway vicious spirals in which every actor has to run faster and faster just to stay in the same place. Still others lure individual actors into doing what seems right locally, which eventually, however, causes suffering for all. Some of the system archetypes that have the broadest relevance include:

Balancing Process with Delay. In this archetype, decision makers fail to appreciate the time delays involved as they move toward a goal. As a result, they overshoot the goal and may even produce recurring cycles. A classic example is real estate developers who keep starting new projects until the market has gone soft, by which time an eventual glut is guaranteed by the properties still under construction.

Limits to Growth. A reinforcing cycle of growth grinds to a halt, and may even reverse itself, as limits are approached. The limits can be resource constraints or external or internal responses to growth. Classic examples include product life cycles that peak prematurely due to poor quality or service, the growth and decline of communication in a management team, and the spread of a new movement.

Shifting the Burden. A short-term "solution" is used to correct a problem, with seemingly happy immediate results. As this correction is used more and more, fundamental long-term corrective measures are used less. Over time, the mechanisms of the fundamental solution may atrophy or become disabled, leading to even greater reliance on the symptomatic solution. A classic example is using corporate human resource staff to solve local personnel problems, thereby keeping managers from developing their own interpersonal skills.

Eroding Goals. When all else fails, lower your standards. This is like "shifting the burden," except that the short-term solution involves letting a fundamental goal, such as quality standards or employee morale standards, atrophy. A classic example is a company that responds to delivery problems by continually upping its quoted delivery times.

Escalation. Two people or two organizations, who each see their welfare as depending on a relative advantage over the other, continually react to the other's advances. Whenever one side gets ahead, the other is threatened, leading it to act more aggressively to reestablish its advantage, which threatens the first side, and so on. Classic examples include the arms race, gang warfare, and price wars.

Tragedy of the Commons.[26] Individuals keep intensifying their use of a commonly available but limited resource until all individuals start to experience severely diminishing returns. Classic examples include sheepherders who keep increasing their flocks until they overgraze the common pasture, and divisions in a firm that share a common sales force and compete for the use of sales reps by upping their sales targets until the sales force burns out from overextension.

Growth and Underinvestment. Rapid growth approaches a limit that could be eliminated or pushed into the future, but only by aggressive investment in physical and human capacity. Eroding goals or standards cause investment that is too weak or too slow, and customers become increasingly unhappy, slowing demand growth and thereby making the needed investment (apparently) unnecessary or impossible. A classic example is countless once-successful growth firms that allowed product or service quality to erode and were unable to generate enough revenues to invest in remedies.

The archetype template is a specific tool that is helping managers identify archetypes operating in their own strategic areas.[27] The template shows the basic structural form of the archetype but lets managers fill in the variables of their own situation. For example, the template of shifting the burden involves two balancing processes that compete for control of a problem symptom. The upper, symptomatic solution provides a short-term fix that will make the problem symptom disappear for a while. The lower, fundamental solution provides a more enduring solution.

Several years ago, a team of managers from a leading consumer goods producer used the archetype of shifting the burden in a revealing way. The problem on which they focused was financial stress, which could be dealt with in two different ways: by running marketing promotions (the symptomatic solution) or by product innovation (the fundamental solution). Marketing promotions were easy to launch. The company was expert in their design and implementation. The results were highly predictable. Product innovation was slow and much less predictable, and the company had a history over the past ten years of product innovation mismanagement. However, only through innovation could it reestablish its leadership position in its industry, which had slid over the past ten to twenty years. What the managers saw clearly was that the more skillful they became at promotions, the more they shifted the burden away from product innovation. However, what really hit home was when one member identified the unintended side effect: the last three CEOs had all come from the advertising function, which had become the politically dominant function in the corporation, thereby institutionalizing the symptomatic solution. Unless the political values shifted back toward product and process innovation, the managers realized, the firm's decline would accelerate—which is just what has happened over the past several years.

Charting Strategic Dilemmas

Management teams typically come unglued when confronted with core dilemmas. A classic example was the way in which U.S. manufacturers faced the low cost–high quality choice. For years, most assumed that it was necessary to choose between the two. Not surprisingly, given the short-term pressures perceived by most managements, the prevailing choice was low cost. Firms that chose high quality usually perceived themselves as aiming exclusively for a high-quality, high-price market niche. The consequences of this perceived either–or choice have been disastrous, and even fatal, as U.S. manufacturers have encountered increasing international competition from firms that have chosen to consistently improve quality and cost.

In a recent book, Charles Hampden-Turner presents a variety of tools for helping management teams confront strategic dilemmas creatively.[28] He summarizes the process in seven steps:

- *Eliciting the Dilemmas*. Identifying the opposed values that form the "horns" of the dilemma; for example, cost as opposed to quality, or local initiative as opposed to central coordination and control. Hampden-Turner suggests that humor can be a distinct asset in this process since "the admission that dilemmas even exist tends to be difficult for some companies."
- *Mapping*. Locating the opposing values as two axes and helping managers identify where they see themselves, or their organization, along the axes.
- *Processing*. Getting rid of nouns to describe the axes of the dilemma. Present participles formed by adding "ing" convert rigid nouns into processes that imply movement. For example, central control versus local control becomes "strengthening national office" and "growing local initiatives." This loosens the bond of implied opposition between the two values. Thus, it becomes possible to think of "strengthening national services from which local branches can benefit."
- *Framing/Contextualizing*. Further softening the adversarial structure among different values by letting "each side in turn be the frame or context for the other." This shifting of the figure–ground relationship undermines any implicit attempts to hold one value as intrinsically superior to the other and thereby to become mentally closed to creative strategies for the continuous improvement of both.

- *Sequencing.* Breaking the hold of static thinking. Very often, values like low cost and high quality appear to be in opposition because we think in terms of a point in time, not in terms of an ongoing process. For example, a strategy of investing in new process technology and developing a new production-floor culture of worker responsibility may take time and money in the near term yet reap significant long-term financial rewards.

- *Waving/Cycling.* Sometimes the strategic path toward improving both values involves cycles in which both values will appear to get worse for a time. However, at a deeper level, learning is occurring that will cause the next cycle to reach a higher plateau for both values.

- *Synergizing.* Achieving synergy where significant improvement is occurring along all axes of all relevant dilemmas. (This is the ultimate goal, of course.) Synergy, as Hampden-Turner points out, is a uniquely systemic notion, coming from the Greek *syn-ergo* or "work together."

NOTES

1. P. Senge, *The Fifth Discipline: The Art and Practice of the Learning Organization* (New York: Doubleday/Currency, 1990).

2. A. P. de Geus, "Planning as Learning," *Harvard Business Review* (March-April 1988): 70–74.

3. All unattributed quotes are from personal communications with the author.

4. B. Domain, *Fortune,* 3 July 1989, pp. 48–62.

5. The distinction between adaptive and generative learning has its roots in the distinction between what C. Argyris and D. Schon have called "single-loop" learning, in which individuals or groups adjust their behavior relative to fixed goals, norms, and assumptions; and "double-loop" learning, in which goals, norms, and assumptions, as well as behavior, are open to change (see, e.g., C. Argyris and D. Schon, *Organizational Learning: A Theory-in-Action Perspective* [Reading, Mass.: Addison-Wesley, 1978]).

6. G. Stalk, Jr., "Time: The Next Source of Competitive Advantage," *Harvard Business Review* (July-August 1988): 41–51.

7. Senge, *Fifth Discipline.*

8. The principle of creative tension comes from Robert Fritz's work on creativity. See R. Fritz, *The Path of Least Resistance* (New York: Ballantine, 1989) and *Creating* (New York: Ballantine, 1990).

9. M. L. King, Jr., "Letter from Birmingham Jail," *American Visions,* January-February 1986, pp. 52–59.

10. E. Schein, *Organizational Culture and Leadership* (San Francisco: Jossey-Bass, 1985). Similar views have been expressed by many leadership theorists. For example, see: P. Selznick, *Leadership in Administration* (New York: Harper and Row, 1957); W. Bennis and B. Nanus, *Leaders* (New York: Harper and Row, 1985); and N. M. Tichy and M. A. Devanna, *The Transformational Leader* (New York: Wiley, 1986).

11. Selznick, *Leadership.*

12. J. W. Forrester, "A New Corporate Design," *Sloan Management Review* (Fall 1965): pp. 5–17 (formerly *Industrial Management Review*).

13. See, for example, H. Mintzberg, "Crafting Strategy," *Harvard Business Review* (July-August 1987): 66–75.

14. R. Mason and I. Mitroff, *Challenging Strategic Planning Assumptions* (New York: Wiley, 1981), p. 16.

15. P. Wack, "Scenarios: Uncharted Waters Ahead," *Harvard Business Review* (September-October 1985): 73–89.

16. De Geus, "Planning as Learning."

17. M. de Pree, *Leadership Is an Art* (New York: Doubleday, 1989), p. 9.

18. For example, see T. Peters and N. Austin, *A Passion for Excellence* (New York: Random House, 1985) and J. M. Kouzes and B. Z. Posner, *The Leadership Challenge* (San Francisco: Jossey-Bass, 1987).

19. I. Mitroff, *Break-Away Thinking* (New York: Wiley, 1988), pp. 66–67.

20. R. K. Greenleaf, *Servant Leadership: A Journey into the Nature of Legitimate Power and Greatness* (New York: Paulist Press, 1977).

21. L. Miller, *American Spirit: Visions of a New Corporate Culture* (New York: Morrow, 1984), p. 15.

22. These points are condensed from the practices of the five disciplines examined in Senge (1990).

23. The ideas below are based to a considerable extent on the work of Chris Argyris, Donald Schon, and their Action Science colleagues: C. Argyris and D. Schon, *Organizational Learning: A Theory-in-Action Perspective* (Reading, Mass.: Addison-Wesley, 1978); C. Argyris, R. Putnam, and D. Smith, *Action Science* (San Francisco: Jossey-Bass, 1985); C. Argyris, *Strategy, Change, and Defensive Routines* (Boston: Pitman, 1985); and C. Argyris, *Overcoming Organizational Defenses* (Englewood Cliffs, N.J.: Prentice-Hall, 1990).

24. I am indebted to Diana Smith for the summary points below.

25. The system archetypes are one of several systems diagraming and communication tools. See D. H. Kim, "Toward Learning Organizations: Integrating Total Quality Control and Systems Thinking" (Cambridge, Mass.: MIT Sloan School of Management, Working Paper No. 3037-89-BPS, June 1989).

26. This archetype is closely associated with the work of ecologist Garrett Hardin, who coined its label: G. Hardin, "The Tragedy of the Commons," *Science,* 13 December 1968.

27. These templates were originally developed by Jennifer Kemeny, Charles Kiefer, and Michael Goodman of Innovation Associates, Inc., Framingham, Mass.

28. C. Hampden-Turner, *Charting the Corporate Mind* (New York: Free Press, 1990).

29. M. Sashkin and W. W. Burke, "Organization Development in the 1980s" and "An End-of-the-Eighties Retrospective," in *Advances in Organization Development,* ed. F. Masarik (Norwood, N.J.: Ablex, 1990).

30. E. Schein (1985).

9

Assessing the Critical Thinking Capability of Your Organization

In this chapter we will attempt to provide you with tools to enable you to assess the critical thinking capability of your organization. These question- naires were designed to be used by our clients and have proved to be very useful in determining whether there is a "need" to do some training or development of your people in any of the three areas of critical thinking.

WHAT IS THE STRATEGIC QUOTIENT OF YOUR ORGANIZATION?

If you are interested in assessing your organization's strategic skill, you may wish to answer the following questions and have your direct reports do the same.

1. Do you have a well-articulated, clear statement of strategy and business con- cept?

    Yes ☐   No ☐

2. Could you write a one- or two-sentence statement of that strategy?

    Yes ☐   No ☐

3. Do your key subordinates understand that strategy?

    Yes ☐   Somewhat ☐   No ☐

4. Could each of your subordinates write a one- or two-sentence statement of that strategy without consulting you or each other?

One Person Could ☐   Some Could ☐   None Could ☐

5. Do they use this statement as a guide for the choices they make in pursuing products, markets, and customers?

Use Frequently ☐   Use Sometimes ☐   Never Use ☐

6. Is it effective in helping you to choose or reject products, markets, and customers?

Very Effective ☐   Somewhat Effective ☐   Not Effective ☐

7. Have you ever sat down as a management team to try to obtain consensus as to the future direction of your firm?

Yes ☐   No ☐

8. Was consensus obtained or are there still different visions of what the organization is trying to become?

Total Consensus   Some Consensus   Little Consensus
(Single Vision) ☐   (Fuzzy Vision) ☐   (Different Visions)☐

9. Is the organization moving in a clear direction?

Yes ☐   Not Sure ☐   No ☐

10. Do you have a separate process of strategic thinking to determine *what* you want to become as opposed to *how* you get there?

Yes ☐   No ☐

11. What is your business concept?

_____

_____

_____

If all the answers are similar and each person's definition of your business concept is identical, then you are in good shape. The wider the discrepancies in their replies compared to yours, the less clear is your strategy. In this case, you may wish to read the following few chapters.

ASSESSING THE INNOVATIVE THINKING OF YOUR ORGANIZATION

If you are interested in doing a diagnostic of the innovative prowess of your organization, the following tool will help. Simply have your entire organization respond to the following questionnaire and then do a tally by level, by function, and/or by department.

1. How frequently are you approached with truly innovative ideas?

   Daily ☐   Monthly ☐   Less than monthly ☐   Never ☐

2. What parts of the business generate the most of the innovative ideas?

   _____
   _____
   _____

3. What do most innovative ideas attempt to improve?

   Marketing ☐   Sales ☐   Operations ☐   Finance ☐   Service ☐
   Productivity ☐   Competitive advantage ☐   Other: _____

4. What is senior management's reaction to innovative ideas?

   Embrace and implement ☐   Study and analyze ☐   Delay ☐
                    Ignore ☐   Reject ☐

5. How does the organization view change?

   As a threat ☐   As an opportunity ☐   As largely irrelevant ☐

6. How does the organization evaluate new ideas?

   Using preestablished criteria ☐   Using situational criteria ☐
   Looking for precedent ☐   By who supports it ☐   By politics ☐

7. How many new ideas or specific improvements have you seen implemented within the organization during the past 12 months?

_____

_____

_____

8. How would you rate your organization's innovation against the direct competition?

Far more innovative ☐   Slightly more innovative ☐   Same ☐
Slightly less innovative ☐   Far less innovative ☐   Can't tell ☐

9. What is the single major factor responsible for getting an innovative idea accepted and implemented within your organization?

_____

10. Considering the environment business climate, and competition, how will your organization have to manage innovation in the next two to three years?

About the same as now ☐   Slightly more aggressively than now ☐
Far more aggressively than now ☐   Less aggressively than now ☐

11. As of now, how likely is it that your organization will attain your answer to no. 10?

Certain ☐   Likely ☐   Possible ☐   Toss-up ☐   Unlikely ☐   Remote ☐

12, What is the percentage of management attention spent on problem solving and innovation, respectively (total must equal 100 percent)?

_____   percent problem solving
_____   percent innovation
100 percent

13. To what extent would you favor a formalized focus on innovation?

Very much ☐   Somewhat ☐   Don't know ☐   Not at all ☐

14. What would be the biggest advantage in emphasizing innovation?

_____

_____

_____

15. What would be the biggest disadvantage in emphasizing innovation?

_____

_____

_____

16. Ideally, where should the focus of innovative approaches be in the organization?

_____

_____

17. What is the biggest obstacle to implementing new ideas within the organization?

_____

_____

_____

18. How willing would you be to participate in an organizational effort to enhance innovation?

Very willing ☐   Agreeable ☐   Depends on the approach ☐   Unwilling ☐

19. What percentage of people do you feel would benefit from a systematic approach to generating innovative ideas and establishing a more innovative climate?

____% of manager   ____% of technical/professional   ____% of administrative
____% of executive   ____% of hourly   ____% of other:_____

20. Please use this space to make any additional comments about innovation and its implications and effects for this organization.

_____

_____

_____

_____

_____

ASSESSING THE DECISION-MAKING ABILITY OF YOUR ORGANIZATION

This questionnaire is designed as a tool to assess the decision-making capability of people in your organization. By having all managers and supervisors respond to this questionnaire, you will be able to construct a profile of your organization's decision-making capability. This profile will allow you to determine:

- If there is a need for decision-making processes,
- At what levels of the organization the need exists, and
- Which process might best apply.

To what degree do your subordinates:

- Have difficulty identifying problems?

Little   *Greatly*
   0   1   2   3   4   5   6   7   8   9   10

- Jump to preconceived causes/solutions of a problem?

Little   *Greatly*
   0   1   2   3   4   5   6   7   8   9   10

- Treat the effects of a problem rather than the cause?

Little   *Greatly*
   0   1   2   3   4   5   6   7   8   9   10

- Focus on blame rather than cause?

Little   *Greatly*
   0   1   2   3   4   5   6   7   8   9   10

- Lack a defined process for problem solving?

Little   *Greatly*
   0   1   2   3   4   5   6   7   8   9   10

- Forget to formulate criteria for decisions?

Little   *Greatly*
   0   1   2   3   4   5   6   7   8   9   10

- Jump to pet alternatives?

Little   *Greatly*
   0   1   2   3   4   5   6   7   8   9   10

- Forget to evaluate risks?

Little   *Greatly*
   0   1   2   3   4   5   6   7   8   9   10

• Have difficulty explaining the rationale behind their decisions?

Little   *Greatly*
    0   1   2   3   4   5   6   7   8   9   10

• Lack a defined process for decision making?

Little   *Greatly*
    0   1   2   3   4   5   6   7   8   9   10

• Forget to anticipate potential problems when implementing a decision?

Little   *Greatly*
    0   1   2   3   4   5   6   7   8   9   10

• Focus on contingent rather than preventive actions?

Little   *Greatly*
    0   1   2   3   4   5   6   7   8   9   10

• Lack a defined process for implementing plans or decisions?

Little   *Greatly*
    0   1   2   3   4   5   6   7   8   9   10

• Fail to generate new or different alternatives?

Little   *Greatly*
    0   1   2   3   4   5   6   7   8   9   10

• Fail to be innovative or imaginative?

Little   *Greatly*
    0   1   2   3   4   5   6   7   8   9   10

• Lack a common approach within the organization to address problems and decisions?

No Process   *Common Process*
    0   1   2   3   4   5   6   7   8   9   10

- What are the obstacles that prevent people from solving problems effectively?

_____
_____
_____
_____

- What are the obstacles that prevent people from making effective decisions?

_____
_____
_____
_____

Although we have attempted to present the above questionnaires in a manner that they can be used "as is," it is difficult to explain how to "read" all the nuances of the answers that will surface.

SUMMARY

Thinking, unlike what most people may believe, does not occur naturally in an organization. In fact, the opposite is usually more accurate. Most people do not think—they simply address situations by shooting from the hip—cowboy style. Common sense is not common practice in many organizations.

If there is a desire to instill sound critical thinking skills in an organization, steps must be taken to ensure that it occurs. Furthermore, if to occur consistently, a structured implementation methodology must be followed. Human beings are indeed creatures of habits—bad habits.

Index

About the Author

MICHEL ROBERT is founder of Decision Processes International, a Westport, Connecticut, consulting firm with partners and offices in 14 countries. It specializes in helping organizations and offices improve the quality of their strategic and operational decisions. He is the author of three books, including *The Strategist CEO: How Visionary Executives Build Organizations* (Quorum, 1988).